One Hispanic Man's Journey

Benito Casados

DEDICATION

This book is dedicated to the many people with whom I have been associate through my entire life.

To my parents who tenaciously struggled their entire life and provided guidance and support throughout my childhood.

To the teacher in both my elementary and secondary schools who always made me aware of their expectations of me and motivated me to excel in my endeavors.

To my family for their constant support, who patiently endured my regular absences from home required by my chosen line of work.

To my two daughters Michelle and Christine for their tolerance of my frequent absences from home

To all my friends, coworkers and colleagues at NASA Space mobile, at JPL, at Optical Data and at Hughes Aircraft Galaxy Classroom.

All have enriched my life and have contributed to the joys and experiences that have been part of my journey in life.

One Hispanic Man's Journey From Northern NM To The Planets.

INTRODUCTION

Each person's life is a true journey. I have been most fortunate in having some interesting opportunities and events in my journey. As you will discover my life originated under most humble beginnings. And perhaps because of this beginning my reflections of events in my journey seem to have additional significance. I have tremendous admiration and appreciation for all those people who had such a positive influence in my life, my parents, my teachers, and members of me extended family. From them I developed self-discipline which in many instances sustained me through some trying times and challenges in work and in life. My work as a science teacher at the Northern New Mexico Normal School was a most rewarding experience. I maintain contact with some of my former students. My employment with NASA placed me in the company of many famous scientists, astronauts and in close proximity of earth shaking events such as the launch of Apollo 11 and the first soft landings on the moon and on the planet Mars. For a kid that came from a large family, a small rural village, with very limited exposure to life, I had to pinch myself when I was making the Spanish television commentary for the worldwide Televisa network in Mexico City. I had been assigned to describe in Spanish the events of the first landing of the Viking I Spacecraft on the planet Mars in the very early morning of July 20,1971. I was 35 years old.

The age of the seventies was the age of the planetary exploration. I was involved in communicating to the educational community the science acquired by the landings on Mars and flyby missions of the Voyager planetary spacecraft to Jupiter, Saturn and Uranus.

Those were exciting times. The nation's space program made many discoveries and accumulated a vast collection of knowledge of our solar system, I was lucky to be involved in these historical events.

CHAPTER 1

Welcome to the Planet Park View

It was cold day with a howling wind blowing from the north on the fourth day of November in 1936. On this day, Roosevelt had just been elected President of the United States for his second term° The people were excited and hopeful even though the country was in the midst of The Great Depression. The nation was going through a period of unprecedented decline in economic activity. It is generally agreed to have occurred between 1929 and 1939. Although parts of the economy had begun to recover by 1936 high unemployment persisted until the Second World War. It probably was not the best time to be having babies but this was the day I was born°

My parents and my four siblings had come in from a remote ranch where they lived 30 miles away to my grandparents' home in the small village of Park View New Mexico. Now called Los Ojos. They were there to await my arrival my parents' fifth child and more importantly to be near a doctor for my expectant mother. When the hour of my birth arrived, the local doctor was called to my grandparents' home to assist in the delivery. There were no hospitals in the area the nearest hospital was one hundred miles away in Santa Fe. Home deliveries were standard with the aid of a midwife or if available a doctor. Now, there was a doctor in this small village. He must have been a devout Democrat. My mother told me that when he whacked me on the butt to launch my first breath he exclaimed "another vote for Roosevelt°". With that anointment I came into this world as a Democrat and I have remained a Democrat for my entire life.

After a few days of recovery, the first order of business was my baptism. My parents selected my Uncle Tony and his wife my Tia Maria as my godparents.

In those days, the godparents selected the name of the newborn. They selected the name Benito and only Benito no middle name. My Tia Maria liked the diminutive name because it could not be easily changed. A few days later, my father packed the family and me, a newborn baby into a mule driven wagon. We headed cross country 30 miles west, back to La Jara ranch which was located in the heart of the Jicarilla Apache Indian Reservation.

CHAPTER 2

The La Jara Homestead

My great grandfather whose name was Antonio Nerio de Jesus Casados was born on January 7th, 1841 in Chamita New Mexico a community in the Espanola valley. He was granted a homestead ranch of 160 acres in 1897 located about 20 miles west of the town of Dulce, New Mexico and signed by President William McKinley. Since the Jicarilla Reservation had been established in 1887 the ranch was located in the middle of the reservation. Evidently in those days it was standard practice to grant homesteads in reservation lands. During this period, several Hispanic people also established homestead ranches in this area. The homestead document granting my great grandfather, Nerio de Jesus Casados, 169-acre land grant signed by President William McKinley, in 1897.

The United States of America,

To all to whom these Presents shall come, Greeting:

Whereas, There has been deposited in the General Land Office of the United States a Certificate of the Register of the Land Office at *Clayton New Mexico Territory*, whereby it appears that, pursuant to the Act of Congress approved 20th May, 1862, "To secure Homesteads to actual Settlers on the Public Domain," and the acts supplemental thereto, the claim of *Nerio Casado* has been established and duly consummated, in conformity to law, for the *South half of the North East quarter and the North half of the South East quarter of section five in Township twenty-four North of Range thirty-four East of New Mexico Meridian in New Mexico Territory containing one hundred and sixty acres*

according to the Official Plat of the Survey of said Land, returned to the General Land Office by the Surveyor General.

Now know ye, that there is, therefore, granted by the United States unto the said *Nerio Casados* the tract of Land above described: To have and to hold the said tract of Land, with the appurtenances thereof, unto the said *Nerio Casados* and to *his* heirs and assigns forever; subject to any vested and accrued water rights for mining, agricultural, manufacturing, or other purposes, and rights to ditches and reservoirs used in connection with such water rights as may be recognized and acknowledged by the local customs, laws, and decisions of courts; and also subject to the right of the proprietor of a vein or lode to extract and remove his ore therefrom, should the same be found to penetrate or intersect the premises hereby granted, as provided by law, and there is reserved from the lands hereby granted, a right of way thereon for ditches or canals constructed by the authority of the United States.

In testimony whereof, I, *William McKinley*, PRESIDENT OF THE UNITED STATES OF AMERICA, have caused these letters to be made Patent, and the Seal of the General Land Office to be hereunto affixed.

Given under my hand, at the City of Washington, the *twentieth* day of *October*, in the year of our Lord one thousand eight hundred and *Ninety seven*, and of the Independence of the United States the *one hundred and*

By the President: *William McKinley*

By *F. M. McKean*

D. H. Brush Secretary.

Recorder of the General Land Office.

My father his two brothers and two sisters grew up on this ranch. It was a beautiful place. La Jara Lake was a sizeable body of water that not only made the setting breath taking but it provided moisture to the surrounding acreage yielding an abundant crop of hay and a most generous garden.

It was on this Indian land that my father was raised. Here is where he brought my mother to live once they were married.

My parents were married in 1928. My mother was a resident of Park View and my dad was raised in La Jara ranch 30 miles west of Park View. I have no idea how they met. I suspect it happened at the traditional Saturday night dance. My father was not a religious person so I don't imagine they met in mass or any other religious event. Another possibility for meeting may have been some relative's wedding. After a brief courtship they were married in Park View on February 26, 1928. My father was born in 1905 he was twenty-three-year-old my mother was 21. Following the wedding my dad placed his bride in a horse drawn wagon and headed west to La Jara Ranch thirty miles away. It was a cross country trip no roads and it must have been quite a rough wagon trip on a cold winter day°

La Jara Ranch was in the middle what is now the Jicarilla Apache Reservation. In 1897 my great grandfather was granted a homestead of 160 acres. This occurred after the Jicarilla Apaches were granted their reservation in 1887.

The reservation was expanded in 1907 to include land more conducive to ranching and agriculture and within several decades realized the rich natural resources of the San Juan Basin under the reservation land. Today the reservation has a land area of 1,364,046 sq mi 3,532,864 km2 and had a population of 3. 300. The Jicarilla Apache Nation as it is known today is one of the richest in the country. It has vast fields of oil natural gas and coal. Most of its people receive generous grants from the royalties of these resources and live in the tribal headquarters community of Dulce near the reservation northern end.

Passed on May 20, 1862 the Homestead Act accelerated the settlement of the western territory by granting adult heads of families 160 acres of surveyed public land for a minimal filing fee and 5 years of continuous residence on that land. The Homestead Act enacted during the Civil War in 1862 provided that any adult citizen or intended citizen who had never borne arms against the U. S. government could claim 160 acres of surveyed government land. Claimants were required to "improve" the plot by building a dwelling and cultivating the land. After 5 years on the land the original filer was entitled to the property free and clear except for a small registration fee. Title could also be acquired after only a 6-month residency and trivial improvements provided the claimant paid the government §1. 25 per acre. After the Civil War Union soldiers could deduct the time they had served from the residency requirements.

After the enactment of the Homestead Act many Hispanic ranchers homesteaded land in Northern New Mexico and made a comfortable living by planting wonderful gardens and raising and selling cattle sheep goats and horses.

My great grandfather established a magnificent ranch in his homestead property in close proximity of La Jara Lake. This natural lake fed moisture to the surrounding land yielding abundant grazing and hay. Additionally, my parents grew a great garden where potatoes beans and other staple vegetables were grown.

Since the majority of the population was Apache Indians, they were regular visitors at my parents' home. My parent had an ice cream maker and from time to time my mother would make a gallon of ice cream which was a great hit and novelty for the local Apache Indians.

My cousins from Park View would sometime spend time at the ranch. My mother told me a story of an incident that occurred when one of my cousins was visiting. A young Indian came by for a visit and was comfortably seated in the kitchen. His entire attire consisted of a "loin cloth". My cousin kept staring having never seen a man in a loin cloth before.

The Indian became self-conscious because of this staring youngster and asks my mother. "why is your nephew looking looking and looking at me" To which my mother responded, "he wonders how you manage cold temperatures without clothes". The Indian then looked at my cousin, took his hand and touched his face and said, "just like your face the same for my butt" In other words you survive without covering your face the same goes for my butt.

The ranch was isolated. The nearest grocery store was in Dulce New Mexico about 20 miles away. All the roads were dirt roads and were quite impassable during the rainy season and impossible in the winter months. There were no medical services and most importantly there were no schools. Consequently, my father and his siblings had no formal education. I remember asking my father how much time did he spend in school. He had a vague recollection of a traveling teacher that made the rounds. His assessment of his total education was around three weeks of instruction. My father could read and write in Spanish. I suspect my mother may have been his teacher. He learned to speak a little English. I would not say he was fluent but he spoke enough to conduct business. My father had two brothers and two sisters. Their mother my grandmother died in 1918 during the devastating influenza epidemic. My Father was about 13 years old at the time of his mother's death. My father had a tough childhood. I am told that my grandfather was a hard man. One of my uncles left home when he turned twenty-one. The story told is that my grandfather would hire him out to local ranchers and he would pocket his earnings. My uncle understandably was not happy with that arrangement. Being the respectful son that he was when he turned twenty-one he saddled his horse and quietly left home. He returned to visit our family about forty years later. My father could never comprehend the concept of playing and having "fun". As a child and as an adult he had worked all his life. He never owned a toy baseball basketball and football were totally foreign to him.

I mentioned earlier the absence of schools in the area. The young Native Americans were shipped to the Santa Fe Indian School to attend a K-12 boarding school operated by the Bureau of Indian Affairs. Another choice was St. Catherine Indian School a Catholic Indian school operated by an order of nuns.

Since my father and his family were not of Indian descent they were not eligible to attend Indian schools. Additionally, the need for education was not fully appreciated by my grandfather's generation. Bottom line, my father grew up totally uneducated. My mother whose maiden name was Madrid was born in Park View. Fortunately for her there was an elementary school in the "town" of Park View. My mother graduated from the 8th grade. She could write and speak English as well as Spanish.

Memories of a young boy living in La Jara Ranch:
By my brother, Ross Casados (1930-2018)

I was seven years old and my brother Pablo was nine years old. I have a vague recollection of what it was to live out there in the middle of nowhere. There were no kids nearby to play with, exception for an occasional visit from our Jicarilla Indian neighbors, who came to have their wagons fixed. My father was an accomplished blacksmith.

Other people stopped by on their way to Colorado. There was plenty of room for guests to stay over as long as they wanted. The ranch house consisted of seven rooms. It was a big adobe house. My great grandfather put a lot of hard work in building this house. I remember this was a time when we were quite happy. I do not remember hardships of any kind. My older brother Pablo was old enough to be able to ride a horse, named Shark. He took care of the cattle out in the range. Even though we grazed our cattle on Indian land, they never prohibited us from grazing our livestock.

My dad also raised hogs. I was in charge of feeding them. In early summer the hogs were turned loose during the summer. There was an abundance of scrub oaks that yielded generous amounts of acorn on which the hogs loved and feasted on it all summer. After being loose and surviving all summer in September and October the hogs started coming back to the ranch.

The sows would lead their piglets back to familiar sheds. I remember the Indians owned a large bore hog that traveled all over the range. He was a huge beast that stood about four feet tall and probably weighed a thousand pounds. My father had to chase him of the ranch on horseback. Even then he charged the horse he was a mean hog! He would go into the potato patch and eat our potatoes. The potatoes patch was about an acre and produced several tons of potatoes. My dad would sell the potatoes to the locals and to the store in Dulce. The ground was fertile and produced large potatoes, some of them weighed a pound. My brother Pablo and I would sort potatoes by size for sale and storage. Our ranch produced corn, peas, and other vegetables which my mother canned. We had an underground cellar for food storage. There was no electricity in those days and we did not own a refrigerator. My father made an icebox. Blocks of ice were placed in the icebox to keep from spoiling. In the winter ice was harvested from La Jara Lake and stored in the icehouse. The ice was covered with sawdust to prevent it from melting.

Come haying season, I remember how part of the hay was baled into eighty pound bales. The baled hay was sold and the loose hay that was stacked was kept to feed the cattle and horses through the winter months.

The process of baling hay was a wonder to behold. My grandfather was a real skilled craftsman. He built a hay baler from "scratch." Were he had the knowledge to build this baler is beyond me. It was powered by a team of horses moving in a circle to stretch out a big spring. When the cycle was completed the spring would release and push the plunger with hay in front into the square chamber. A bale divider was inserted every forty inches to make the bale. It was considered a good day if they baled 100 bales in a single day.

There were rattlesnakes at La Jar Ranch! This made for dangerous surroundings. Fortunately we were never bitten by a rattlesnake. My sister Belinda was about three years old, while playing in the front yard a rattlesnake came within three feet of her. My Dad saw the snake and came to the rescue by killing the snake on the spot.

Another memorable event at the ranch was the bathing of a large number of sheep. Every year the herds came up with an infectious skin disease. It was contagious and the sheep had to be treated. The cure was to dip in sheep in tank about 4 feet by 5 feet by 4 feet. The bathing solution was water with sulfur. The bathing occurred after the sheep were sheared.

In 1931 on the 19th of November the region experienced a horrendous snowstorm. In a period of forty-eight hours, a total of four to five feet of snow covered the area. My Grandfather had a herd of 1500 head of sheep and 800 of them had been moved south about ten miles to the winter grazing area. It was a very wet snow and if froze into a solid blanket of snow making it impossible for the animals to graze, more drastic was the fact that my Father and Grandfather were unable to travel to the area to provide feed for the sheep. Sadly 800 head of ship perished as a result of the storm. Fortunately, 700 head remained at the ranch and survived the great snowstorm of 1931. The total loss of sheep by all the ranchers in the area was close to 50,000 head of sheep. It was indeed a devastating snowstorm for all the local ranchers!

My great Grandfather lived to the age of 95. As a very young child I remember him sitting in front of a wood-burning stove smoking a pipe with his dog at his side. The dog's name was Pope. (Spinglish word for PUPPY). My great grandfather told me a story of how POPE had saved his life from a big black bear that attacked him almost killed him. POPE surprised the bear with a vicious attack; the bear ran away with POPE chasing him. My great grandfather had scars of the bear's claws and bear teeth marks on this head. He was a man five feet five inches tall! I am now 84 years old but I still have fond memories of my growing up days at La Jara Ranch at the Jicarilla Indian Reservation. My family moved away from La Jara ranch in 1938. My father and his two brothers decided to sell the place to the Bureau of Indian Affairs. I never knew the true reason for the sale. I suspect two factors contributed to the decision to sell. One my mother was not enthused about living out in the middle of the reservation away from her parents and other relatives and secondly there were no schools. We were all born two years apart. My oldest brother Paul was ten years old. I was eight years old my brother Ted was six. I and my older brother would spend the school months with my maternal grandparents in Park View. This was not the most desirable situation for the family.

CHAPTER 3

Northern New Mexico and Southern Colorado - 1875

While doing my research for this book I came across some very interesting articles about as well as a description of life of the Hispanic people that lived in the area and the life of the various Native American tribes. The article was written on July 4 the year was 1875.

THE FAR SOUTHWEST

Sketches of Frontier Life and Scenery in The Mountain Regions of New Mexico.

Tierra Amarilla - Ration Day at an Indian Agency - Navajos Utes and Apaches. The Mode of Life of the Mexicans-Pious Penitentes and Their Sin Expelling Luxuries.

Special Correspondence of the Inter Ocean
Camp on Horse Lake New Mexico July 4, 1875
BY DAVID GREY

We left Tierra Amarilla on the first. but just as we reached this place on the evening of the 2nd one of our wagons broke down making it necessary to remain here for a day or two for other arrangements. Our camp is cozily located on the banks of a beautiful mountain lake the breakdown having occurred at an opportune time and place. I therefore improve the occasion to put on record a few notes regarding TIERRA AMARILLA AND ITS SURROUNDINGS.

This is a Mexican plaza of 200 or 300 inhabitants and it has for many years been an important objective point for various purposes. At one time a small detachment for regular soldiers were stationed there for the purpose of holding the Indians in check. Last season the Wheeler Expedition remained there some time in the performance of sundry scientific work. It was in this vicinity that Professor E. D. Cope. The distinguished paleontologist made many discovered of extinct animals concerning which paragraphs are just now circulating through the newspapers. His preliminary report has but recently been finished. At the present time and Indian agency is established in Tierra Amarilla. The agent in charge is Mr. S. A. Russell late of Des Moines Iows. I found him a most agreeable and intelligent gentleman and he could not well be otherwise for he reads the Inter-Ocean and sundry others of the best journals in the land. He was very useful to me in the way of furnishing information concerning the country and the routes beyond. I had heard very favorable reports concerning him and his official administration of affairs and I found that he fully deserved the excellent reputation he has achieved. I was there on ration day and examined some of the articles which he was engaged in issuing to our brethren. The flour was sweet and good fair quality-good enough for the reader or the writer of these lines. The beef was excellent f know for I saw the animals before they were slaughtered and the beef when it was weighed out. The beef that was issued however" looked somewhat soiled and dirty but this was since from choice the Indians did it themselves and they are not very fastidious in the matter of diet They are very greedy in their desire of the offer and they cannot be kept out of the slaughter yard" while the animals are being butchered without great difficulty. So, to please them and thus secure as much exemption form friction as possible. They are allowed to work at the butchery very much in their own way. Hence the diet but as to the good quality of these staple articles of food there is no question whatever. The flour costs the government seven cents per pound and the beef five cents after it is slaughtered. These prices are certainly very reasonable. As to the tobacco I think it is villainous like all plug tobacco-but the Indians and squaws are nearly crazy to get it and so one else has any right to complain. It was rather and interesting occasion this ISSUING OF RATIONS.

The Indians were out in all their best attire- they had their faces painted and greased. They are mainly Utes but there is also quite a large fraction of Apaches. On this occasion there were twenty-five to forty Navajos, visiting brothers, Mr. Russell informed me. It is customary to issue rations to such casual visitors at all the agencies.

These Navajos are a very cleanly and superior race of Indians- taller lighter - colored and more intellectual than the Utes and Apaches. These last are a pair of filthy and disgusting races. But few of the men were in attendance the work of receiving and carrying off their rations deving mainly upon the women. Those I saw were mostly of very low stature and very repulsive. They dress largely in skins and some of their smoke tanned petticoats had a most ancient and dilapidated look. But it was astonishing how one of these sisters could trip off with 100 pounds of beef dripping over her shoulders. I saw one of these Apaches belles of possibly sweet sixteen who had staggered off with too big a load of beef. She was forced to lay it down by the side of the building and while resting form her burden this Minnehaha was deliberately tearing off and devouring little strips of the bloody beef-taking it very rare. Altogether these women were a set of disgusting hags as one could expect to and in the most degraded and barbarous land under the sun. I think a conscientious agent like my friend Russell who attends to the wants of these Indians nears their complaints and manages to keep them contented and quiet earns all the salary he gets. So far as I could judge, he is doing this duty in a very efficient and conscientious manner and I am glad to be able to say this concerning the first Indian agent I have met out here and proud to say he hails from my own State. The leading mans of this Plaza however is Tom Burns who is well known all through this Territory as well as in Colorado. He has been there some eight or nine years" following the various avocations of merchant stock raiser freighter and general businessman. He is only thirty-five years old but enjoys a wide reputation as a useful" enterprising public-spirited and honorable man. Like most of the Americans who came here and settled at in early day he married a Mexican lady and his choice was one who had enjoyed excellent educational advantages. She is a lady of rare intelligence and refinement. In a business point of view, he has been prosperous and is in the possession of a fair competence which he has earned by his own efforts for he came there poor. Born in Ireland, he possesses all the quick-wit of his race but his is a wit which leaves no sting behind and he is quite as apt to make himself the subject of a joke as anyone else. He dispenses the most liberal and generous hospitality alike to Americans and Mexicans and enjoys the largest respect and esteem of all who know him. During my stay in Tierra Amarilla I was the recipient of many favors at his hands-no more however than he freely accorded to all-and it is with great pleasure that I write these kind words concerning him. I appreciated this more because there are no hotels in this section and very few indeed, who can speak our language or give a traveler any information concerning the country. The reader who strays off to this remote nook will not on all his journey find a more genial and pleasant companion a kind friend in need or a more hospitable gentleman than Thomas D. Bums of Tierra Amarilla.

THE Principal PLAZA Is situated at the upper end of a wide valley through which runs the Chama River a great Wild stream in the seasons of floods but now shrunk to a creek. There are four or five other plazas but that where the Indian agency and Mr. Burns are located is the principal one. It has all the characteristics of these Mexican Huddles the houses are mainly built of adobe mostly with flat roofs and all looking at a little distance as though they might have been intended for forts. Two of three ditches wind lazily through the town for the use of the people there as well as to irrigate the fields below. The houses look very rough on the outside but many of them are clean and tidily kept inside. In fact, it seems to me that the women are generally more industrious and enterprising than their lords. As I have journeyed along I have often had occasion to ask for a drink of water at these Mexican houses. It was always brought to me in a glass or neatly scoured cup- clean sweet and cool.

On many of these occasions I have seen the father of the family crawling out of his blankets on the adobe floor while the wife and everybody else seemed to be hard at work. This was so generally the case that I could not fail to set these men down as decidedly indolent and lazy-due to their Indian blood and their wives the reverse. Tierra Amarilla is truly a frontier town. Rather lively on the days when the Indians are drawing their supplies but dull enough the rest of the time. It rejoices in a profusion of dogs which can beat any other I have ever seen in howling and barking at nights. While I was there somebody was dispensing poison among them with decided results- for they were dying off with an alacrity that pleased me. You see many little children in the streets who are neatly clad and look well as well as numbers who look like so many little Indians-their shirt tails hanging on the outer walls like the banners of Macbeth. Little sandy spotted pigs with snouts preternaturally elongated also abound. The simon-pure Mexican hog" by the way looks very much like the pictures of wild board which we see in the natural histories. They have long noses arched backs tremendous ears and stand high from the ground. You might count their ribs at the distance of a dozen rods.

Tierra Amarilla in addition to other things is the HEADQUARTERS OF A VERY HEAVY WOOL AND CATTLE TRADE. Large flocks and herds are owned by the citizens. They are pastured in the summer in the mountain valleys and are driven south or west for winter pasturage. Thousands are sent into the San Juan region for this purpose and other thousands into regions farther south. You see few Mexican boys around the plaza. Because they are off in the mountains with the flocks and herds. The Jesuit priest complained of

BENITO CASADOS

this as one of the reasons why the boys and young men were growing up in ignorance. I was surprised to learn how wonderfully these little fellows withstand exposure. They are out all summer sleeping on the ground wherever the cold night overtakes them with only one blanket and that by no means thick or heavy. They keep the flocks moving as they exhaust the grass or need water. Today a little valley will be vocal with their songs and shouts and the bleating of the flocks or the lowing of the herds and tomorrow it will be silent and deserted and its vegetation quite exhausted. Often in our journeying along we have made it a point to reach a certain camping place where according to the traditions of the mountain teamsters there was plenty of grass but on reaching the spot have found that the grass had just been eaten to the ground by a herd of these Mexican sheep. The wealth of this country at present is centered in its flocks and herds of which it possesses more than I could possibly estimate. Conejos County Colorado contains 200¨000 to 300¨000 sheep¨ and thousands and thousands of cattle. Surrounding Tierra Amarilla is one of the finest pastoral regions of country in the United States. It is covered with rich blue native grass which is very nutritious and which affords pasturage early in the spring and late in the autumn. This grass would also be excellent for stock all the winter long but for the fact that the snow fall to the depth of three or four feet which makes it impossible for the cattle or sheep to get their own living hence they are sent to other sections where there are no snowfalls.

In that vicinity, also there is SOME OF THE FINEST SCENERY IN THE ROCKY MOUNTAINS. Off to the northwest is Bandit Peak a mountain that raises its granite cones and rugged crags to the height of 14¨000 feet Snow lies upon it now and will until it comes again, next winter. Northeast of the plaza there are a couple of granite peaks separated only by a narrow canon. To the eye, they do not look to be over 600 or 800 feet high but Ueut Morrison of the Wheeler survey who measured the attitude on the 2d instant¨ informed me that they were 2¨400 feet above the general level of

18

the valley. It is now droughty thereabouts but I was told that a beautiful cascade falls from near the top of one of these great granite peaks in the spring and during the rainy season. Its reservoir is a small lake. The water falls so far it reaches the bottom in foam° I regretted that this beautiful waterfall whose track I could see with a glass was not in operation. I may add that these peaks seen near at hand. You would say that you could reach the top of either in an hour. But they are in reality eight or ten miles away. Heavy snow-clad mountains lay further west climbing a high hill south of the plaza you have one of the most splendid views I have yet seen in these mountains. Off to the southwest the vision is unobstructed for eighty to 120 miles. You look out over thousands of acres of pine timber and across broad and elevated plateaus or tablelands" which drop off suddenly into valleys or canons-first a perpendicular wall of lightcolored rock then talus or sloping mass of debris extending out from the base. To the west and northwest far out over upland glade. and glen you are able to see high mountains which it would take you many days and cost you a world of labor even to reach the bases saying nothing of the unparalleled labor of climbing to the summits. Really" these views are not only grand and sublime but in the highest degree romantic and 18 beautiful. Combined with all this mountain scenery the valley looked pleasant and beautiful clad as it was in this emerald vesture of grass and grain. The pine timber in this section is very fine. You see constantly around you outside of the valleys tall pine trees" often thirty to sixty feet to the first limbs[a] and if you have ever had anything to do with lumbering you begin to speculate upon the probable amount of clear stuff they contain. That would be a grand site for a stream of water sawmill but for the most important of all facts- there would be no market for lumber in this greaser land. But one of these days a railroad will penetrate this sleepy village. THE PENITENTE ADMINISTERS THIS Soul-purifying and sin-expelling luxury upon himself. The wool card is fastened upon a stiff strap of leather and they strike themselves such smart blows that it frequently becomes necessary to pick the wires out of the flesh with a knife of other sharp. implement° In some cases these wool cards are made into a girdle which is worn around the waist-doubtless for the expulsion of sins which lurk near the heart. I heard many other strange stories concerning these Penitents but I have given the reader a sufficient idea of the punishments and humiliations which they thus publicly inflict upon themselves with a view to the exorcism of devils or the wiping out of their multifarious sins. As the Catholic priest wield and unbounded influence over these ignorant and half-civilized people it seems to me that they must be in a great degree responsible for these singular customs of their flocks. Now that we have a cardinal in the country and an archbishop in Santa Fe possibly these practices may be overhauled and discontinued They certainly will be when the railroad the school-house the steepled church and the protracted meeting reach the plazas of Conejos Ojo Caliente. Rito. and Tierra Amarilla which they sure to do at no distant period. When that time comes, these senseless practices will be laughed to scorn. David Grey

Such was the view and attitudes of one journalist in 1875. Northern New Mexico and Southern Colorado was a region untamed and populated by Native American tribes of Apaches" Utes and Navajos and of course an emerging population of Hispanic people who originated in Spain and had ended up in Mexico City. From there they moved north via the Santa Fe Trail into Santa Fe. From Santa Fe, they moved to the mountainous northern New Mexico and Southern Colorado to villages such as Tierra Amarilla, Los Ojos and other settlements in Southern Colorado.

CHAPTER 4

The Hispanic Community.

First and foremost, I personally do not like the use of the word Latino when addressing the Spanish speaking population in this country I am a Hispanic person. My ancestors originally came from Spain. I speak Spanish and I do not speak Latin! It is true that Latin is the root language of all romance languages, Spanish, French, Portuguese and Italian. I do not believe the Italian, French and Portuguese people living in this county call themselves or are referred to as Latinos. Therefore, I am imploring the media and politicians to start using the word HISPANIC when referring to those of us who speak the Spanish Language. When I was growing up in New Mexico we were referred by the term of Spanish American. I still prefer that term.

Secondly, all Hispanics that vote in elections are citizens! Immigration is not a major issue for these voters. I hasten to remind Americans that many of the ancestors of Hispanic Americans arrived in this country centuries before many "American" ancestors. Many Hispanic people in the Southwest have been here for many generation. Not all of us arrived from Mexico in the past years. The first member of my family arrived at Santa Fe, New Mexico in 1692 he was a member of the Spanish military. A large segment of the ancestors of the Hispanic population in the southwest arrived in this country during the 15 and 1600s. There is archeological evidence that San Juan del Yunke was established north of Santa Fe, by Spaniards before the establishment of St Augustine in Florida, the oldest city in the United States. While we do have much concern for Hispanic people caught in their strife of undocumented immigration, we are sensitive of the fact that they come here dedicated to work and provide for their families. Their needs in their native countries are so severe that it drives them to enter this country in most instances, illegally. We are concerned about their well-being and we endorse and support a humane solution to the problems of all undocumented workers that are here from many countries.

It is my belief that if we were to provide a work permit that allowed them to move freely between this country and Mexico, the illegal residents would be eliminated and replaced by documented workers. Most Hispanics are very attached to their families. They don't want to be away from their wives and children. This devotion to family is what motivates them to illegally bring their wives and children into this country. A work permit would be a document that would allow the worker to travel freely back to their families and return legally to his or her job. I am quite sure this arrangement would keep families in Mexico their first love!

What is important to Hispanics?

The best description of what Hispanics expect from their government was clearly enunciated by a great Republican president, Abraham Lincoln in his Gettysburg address:

......that this nation, under God, shall have a new birth of freedom -- and that government of the people, by the people, for the people, shall not perish from the earth's

♣ **of the people:** Hispanics want to be included in the democratic process, they want their voices to be heard, and their concerns and issues validated when addressed and acted upon by our government.

♣ **by the people;** Hispanics will continue to give voice to their issues through the ballot box. We will vote for those candidates that illustrate an appreciation for our culture, gain knowledge and concern for the issues that Hispanics face such as health care, education and equal employment opportunities, and equality in the eyes of the law.

♣ **for the people,** Hispanics want a government that is there for the people. A government that looks out and is concerned for the welfare, the education, and the safety and health of all people, rich, poor, white, black, gay, straight, or poke dot. The Hispanic population is not looking for a handout from the government of from any political party. You seldom if ever you see a Hispanic person pan handling at a street corner. Hispanics are a proud and resilient people that care for their families and our fellow human beings. Likewise, they prefer a government and a political party that are sensitive to the needs of all people. The Democratic Party is perceived by Hispanics as being sensitive to the above. If the Republicans try on these issues...maybe a few Hispanics will "migrate" to the Republican party. The Republicans have a lot of work ahead of them. Hispanics deserve and demand to be treated with dignity as a person and respect as citizens. The first poem I learned as a child was the following, and I believe it describes how a person behaves towards government, towards family (parents) and how to treat senior citizens.

Here is a little poem I was taught at a very young age, I call it guiding words for discipline and honorable and respectful behavior!

Respeto a loss superiores	**Respect for your Superiors**
Respeto y amor al Padre	**Respect and love for your Father**
Amor y tiernuda a la Madre Y	**Love and Tenderness for your Mother**
Reverencia a los mayors.	**And Reverence for Senior**

CHAPTER 5

The FIRST CASADOS FAMILY ARRIVES AT SANTA FE NM IN 1694

The Casados family came to New Mexico with other Spanish colonists recruited at Mexico City in 1693. Francisco Lorenzo de Casados was born circa 1670 a native of Cadiz, Spain. In June of 1694 he his wife and a son arrived at Santa Fe along with the other Mexico City Spanish colonists. This family does not appear on the first two known muster rolls of colonists but they were listed on the muster roll made by General Don Juan Paptista Anzaldo De Peralta y Contreras at Zacatecas on November 16, 1693. The scant information provided from this record is his first name Francisco Lorenzo and the mention of his wife and a son both unnamed. Furthermore, a note was written that he was forced to go to New Mexico for ten years by order of the Viceroy of Nueva Espana. A memorial of the colonists forwarded to Governor Vargas by Fray Francisco Farfana in January 1694 provided Francisco Lorenzo's full name with the following information∫ "Francisco Lorenzo de Casados su muger y un nino. " Once again there is a note in the margin of the record stating he was forced to come to New Mexico. At this time, we have no records to inform us about the circumstances which lead to his "exile" however he was most likely sentenced for some infraction of the law. Nonetheless, this information verifies that the Casados family was among those recruited by the command of the Viceroy of Nueva España.

From a later record, we learn that Francisco Lorenzo's wife was Ana Pacheco and that their son Francisco Jose de Casados born circa 1693. This family group does not appear in the census of people receiving livestock from Governor Vargas which was made in 1697. Yet by 1704 Francisco Lorenzo de Casados was a widower and a resident of Santa Fe when he was a witness for the prenuptial investigation of Captain Juan Paez Hurtado and Teodora Garcia de la Riva. Casados' prior acquaintance with Paez Hurtado a leading figure in Santa Fe may have helped in establishing himself among the socially privileged. Although Casados had been exiled to New Mexico this fact did not prevent him from remaining in New Mexico for ten years and then continued to reside in Santa Fe where he was an active member of the Confraternity of San Miguel which ardently worked at restoring the chapel of San Miguel. On May 25 1704 Captain don Francisco Lorenzo de Casados purchased land at Santa Fe from Antonia Fresqui and her children" Sebastian Fresqui Melchora Fresqui and Maria Fresqui. He intended to build a house next to the house of Antonia Fresqui. The following year on September 19"1705 Casados" again, referred to as Captain purchased additional land owned by Juan Robledo that was situated in Santa Fe on "the other side of the river" on September 22, 1713. This particular piece of land was adjoining land of Casados. The other boundaries included the road leading to Alamo lands of Vincente Armijo and the lands of Francisco Perea. Captain Francisco Lorenzo Casados took part in the 1715 campaign against the Farones Apaches and he was described as a settler of Santa Fe who was fully armed and had eight mules with him. This information attests to the fact that he was a man who was worthy of respect as a soldier and as a member of the Santa Fe community. By 1716" Casados was married again unfortunately the name of his second wife is unknown and it is not known if he had any children from the second union.

When Governor Valveerde organized the campaign against the Utes in 1719 Captain Francisco Lorenzo de Casados stated he was a resident of Santa Fe had served the King for twenty-five years and urged that the campaign against the Utes be undertaken due to their robberies insolence and their continued cooperation with the Commanches. He took part in the campaign and when seven of the soldiers became ill he was said to have accidentally discovered a remedy for the swelling that took place on his own face" apparently caused by poison ivy. The soldiers had laid down on the herb or stepped on it and found that it caused their bodies to swell and the skin to peel off with most harm being to their genitals. The remedy discovered accidentally by Casados was to chew chocolate and then to rub saliva from that act on the affected parts.

The Casados surname was passed to Francisco Jose Casados the son of Captain Casados" who was married to Maria Barbara de Archibeque and Antonia Gutierrez. Casados and Archibeque were married at Santa Fe on October 28"1716 with Governor Juan Paez Hurtado and his wife Dona Teodora Garcia de la Riva as witnesses. They were long time residents of Santa Fe and both were still living in 1750 when their family was enumerated in the census of Santa Fe. They had a son named Miguel and this census information provides the names of three other children.

Francisco Jose Casados and Maria Barbara de Archibeque had at least five other children. Francisco Jose appears to have been a prominent citizen of Santa Fe enough so to merit being appointed as Alcalde Mayor of Santa Cruz in 1725. There is no indication that he remained at Santa Cruz for more than one year after which time he returned to Santa Fe. From these original families who started in Santa Fe descendants moved to settle in various communities such as Santa Cruz, Abiqui, Toas , Jemez San Ildefonso" 'communities in the Espanola valley and San Miguel del Vado. My ancestors also moved one hundred and thirty miles north of Santa Fe which resulted in my great grandfather homesteading in the Jicarilla Apache Indian Reservation.

My Childhood home in Park View New Mexico (Los Ojos,NM)

CHAPTER 6

Growing up in Park View Los Ojos

About 1938 my parents and five children moved from La Jara Ranch to Los Ojos is a very small picturesque village situated on Northern mountain in the state of New Mexico. I was two years old. Los Ojos sits on a beautiful spot at an elevation of 7200 feet surrounded by a pine covered ridge.

Most people have the impression that New Mexico is a desert state. A notion developed by driving across New Mexico from east to west on Highway I-40 which replaced the historic Highway. This road has interesting vistas of a vast desert land starting on the New Mexico Texas border interrupted by a few small towns the city of Albuquerque and ending at the eastern Arizona border in Tony Hilleman country and the city of Gallup.

Los Ojos during my childhood was called Park View. The name was appropriate. This quaint village sits on a valley bordered to the east by a ridge or mesa rising about eighty feet above the valley. We called this ridge La Ceja which was covered with a thick forest of Ponderoa Pines. At the base of this rocky ridge many springs of beautiful cool water flows onto the green grasslands that cover the valley. In Spanish, a natural spring is called an Ojo which also means eye. The word for eyebrow is Ceja. So, the logic of these names is La Ceja the brow is above the Ojo the eye the spring.

This village was established in 1800 It was originally settled by Spaniards that came first to Mexico and then migrated north to Nueva España, New Spain New Mexico.

Life in Park View

Park View is a small village sits at the bottom of the Brazos Cliffs. A majestic mountain range that pokes up to the sky to an elevation of 11,500 feet. In winter blizzards, the mountain is not visible. It is shrouded by clouds and flying snow. In the winter, when the sun comes over the Brazos Peak glistens with snow against the blue rocky face of the mountain. Each spring, on the eighth or ninth day of May, like clockwork as the snow melts a lake at the top of the mountain overflows its banks and a beautiful waterfall drapes the mountain side. El Chorro, as the waterfall is called can be seen from the front porches of the homes in Park View. The water from the waterfall flows into the Brazos River. The cascade of El Chorro truly marks the beginning of Spring.

The winters can be brutal in this area. In northern Rio Arriba county, most of the homes are heated by burning wood. With winter temperatures dropping below zero every night it takes a lot of wood to keep the house warm. My father sold wood to the area residents. The country was at war. Most of the men of the community had either volunteered or drafted into the military. So, business is good for my Dad's business.

I grew up in a large family. I had four brothers and four sisters. By today's standards this was a large family. We lived in a neighborhood with our extended family which included most of our first cousins, uncles and aunts. All my adult relatives were authority figures and functions somewhat as surrogate parents.

I am a middle sibling. As I was growing up I always felt somewhat ignored by my parents. Most families develop a pecking order. This pecking order evolves in families in a most natural way and the order is usually re-enforced by parent behavior, who unconsciously promote it. The oldest child is usually at the top of the pecking order. Additionally, parents usually exhibit what I call biased affection. In my family it worked as follows. The oldest child becomes the favorite for no other reason other than he or she is the oldest. If the oldest is a male then the next level is the favorite because she is the oldest daughter. She is entitled to additional attention and emotional support simply because she is the oldest daughter. At the other end of the favoritism scale is the youngest child it does not matter whether it is a boy or a girl. That child gets all the attention for the simple reason the "he or she is the youngest."! So, there I was caught in the middle, no attention from anybody and perfectly situated to wear all the hand me downs from my older brothers. I particularly disliked the old winter jackets, faded, threadbare and ugly.

Another hand me down where chores. Very early I inherited the chores of gathering the eggs, making sure the chicken coop was closed and secure each night. Otherwise skunks and weasels would enter the coop and enjoy a chicken fest. A critical chore was I had, was making sure, there was enough wood chopped and stacked in the porch to last twenty-four hours for cooking and heating. A critical component of this duty was that I had to provide kindling to start the fire in the morning. These tasks had to be performed every single day without exception including Christmas day, fourth of July every day! You are probably wondering what would happen if I failed to perform these tasks. Well my father would not physically whip me but the tongue lashing, I got was sometimes worse. I was described as being lazy, irresponsible and hinging around with my no-good friends playing marbles. I seldom failed in fulfilling my duties, when I did everybody took the liberty to criticize me for my deficit behavior. Being a middle sibling was also being somewhat of an outcast. My older brothers never wanted me around, unless I served some function they were too cool to do. I was allowed to go fishing not to fish I never had a fishing pole. My function was to carry the bait or carry whatever fish they caught. Another function if fulfilled as middle sibling was to serve as model for all my older brothers to practice the art of hair cutting. As my hair was being cut I was surrounded by a laughing audience making comments on my hilarious appearance

CHAPTER 7

Starting on my Educational Road

Coming home from school the wind is almost at blizzard level., the temperature is probably around twenty degrees but with the biting wind it felt like ten below zero. I am leaning into the wind as I walk slowly on my way home from school. I am nine years old and in the third grade. My three older brothers are behind, they don't want the kid brother anywhere near them. It's just not allowed. My older sister is also walking home with her friends and some of her cousins. It is the winter of 1946.

In those days nuns were allowed to teach in public schools. The faculty consisted of six Franciscan nuns some of the nuns were local ladies that had chosen the vocation of of being nuns and returning as teaching nuns.

I was enrolled at the Saint Joseph elementary school in September of 1942. In November of that year I was six years old. St. Joseph's Elementary School was the largest building in our town. It was built by the community using local labor materials and talent. The building consisted of three wondrous architectural levels. Not all served directly in an educational purpose. The basement, as we called it was our auditorium. It was a long dark room with a very low ceiling. A small twelve inch high stage was constructed at the south end of the building. With the low ceiling, tall students could not perform in our school productions unless they played little old men or old ladies. It didn't matter that much these were World War II years and most of our plays consisted of promoting victory gardens. So, we all portrayed roles of talking vegetables crouching behind potatoes carrots or other garden goodies. A good friend of mine played the role of a talking cabbage. "I am a cabbage head as you can see" I never forgot the line and to this day he is still called "cabbage" °

The auditorium was heated by a large wood burning stove that reminded me of a squatty black angus bull. This black stove was as temperamental as a bull. The wind had to be blowing in the right direction to heat up the place. Usually it would simply sit and pour smoke profusely into the hall. The doors would be opened to let the smoke out and the cold in, no telling how many great acting talents were chilled forever in that old cold auditorium. I might add this "basement" was our multipurpose room that provided a place for movies school and community productions and bingos. No chill was ever cold enough to lower the zeal of the bingo fever. Next door was the dining room. Some years hot lunches were served and at times it served as a classroom. My first year of school was in this basement classroom. I remember very little of my education during my first year. But I do remember vividly the delicious aromas that emanated from the nuns' kitchen. One of the nuns was the designated cook and oh what magnificent aromas. Early in my first year I discovered a strategy for legally entering this marvelous kitchen and partaking of these gastronomical wonders that tortured me so. One morning as the sweet aromas hit my sensitive nostrils, I stood up from my desk and complained to the nun of a stomach disorder and pain. She immediately inquired what I had eaten for breakfast. I heed and hawed because I really did want to lie. My mother always insisted we have a full breakfast. So, I simply said I had a pain as though I had a hole in my stomach. That was the best I could do to describe my yearnful appetite in terms of physical malady.

Immediately she took my small hand in hers and led me in the direction of my dreams. We entered the kitchen and there taking cinnamon rolls out of the oven stood Sister Mary Stella. I could tell that she generously sampled here own cooking- she was a bit chubby. They discussed my malady and immediately prescribed a large glass of milk with a cinnamon roll. That was my first encounter with a wonder drug My stomach malady was instantly healed!

On the second level of the building were four large classrooms. Each room housed two grade levels and each room had a large wood burning stove in the corner. I suspect I was a more mature first grader resulting in the nuns recommending I skip the second grade and move on to the third grade.

I must admit that I was quite a sharp student. While in the first grade I distinctly remember sitting on a green bench trying to understand the concept of addition as flash cards were shuffled in front of me. One morning as the nun was drilling us on addition and subtraction in one instant as if I had been struck by lightning I understood the concept of addition subtraction multiplication and division. From that moment, on Arithmetic was a breeze. To my surprise, I could perform all the mathematical functions in my mind.

The nuns were excellent teachers. When I started school, I did not speak English. My parents spoke nothing but Spanish at home and the community was 99. 9 Hispanic. There were two Anglo families one ran the local grocery story and the other was the family of the gentleman that operated the local state fish hatchery. I remember learning enough English quickly so that I understood the lesson being presented. I do not recall lessons to learn English but we were taught how to read in English quite early. Verb tenses did seem to provide a problem for me as I tried to speak English. The nuns never taught the lessons in Spanish even though they were fluent in Spanish. Bilingual education had not been discovered nor was it practiced.

In those days, we were considered Spanish Americans. We had no problem with that label. Our ancestors came from Spain and we were fluent in the Spanish language. I have difficulty with the label "Latino". What is the origin of this label? We certainly do not speak Latin. And while it is true that the French Italian Portuguese and Spanish languages are all rooted in the Latin language Latino does not seem appropriate. I have never observed that French, Italian and Portuguese people are referred to as Latinos° So for the record, I and many of my Spanish speaking colleagues prefer that we be identified as Hispanics. Since we do speak Spanish°

The nuns were wonderful and dedicated teachers. And I might add strict disciplinarians. Our school day started at 8:00 o'clock in the morning by attending mass. The school was next door to the church. After mass, we had religious instruction¨ we called it Catechism. Each night we were assigned about 10 questions and answers we had to memorize for the following morning catechism class. For example, I remember the following What makes a sin mortal And What is meant by the Redemption Memorizing the catechism answers plus a regular load of other academic homework was a real challenge and it embedded on me the value of self-discipline. I consider that a fundamental prerequisite for successful living. It is self-discipline that makes a person get out of bed every morning and get to work or school in time. Self-discipline enables one to control adequate amount of food one eats and how much drink one imbibes. It is through self-discipline that people can be tactful in dealing with our fellow human beings. Yes, I believe self-discipline is the pillar of success in our social life and in the workplace.

We lived about a mile from school. The local bus driver ruled that we did not live did not live far enough to qualify to ride the bus. I always wondered about the rule and for some reason my parents never questioned it. It was particularly tough during the cold winter months. Park View has an elevation of 7300 feet in elevation and the winters are long and cold. Since we had to be in time for mass we left home at about seven fifteen in the morning. It was sunrise and the coldest hour of the morning. Back packs had not been invented so, we carried our books with our bare hands. We never had mittens or gloves. A fact of life we accepted and it never occurred to us that the reason we did not have gloves and mittens were simply that our parents could not afford the luxuries of gloves and mittens.

As previously mentioned the nuns were strict disciplinarians. When I was in the fifth grade the Catechism lesson for that morning was on defacing public property. Nowadays known as Graffiti. The students used to write on the walls of the student outhouses. We did not have plumbing in the school the "bathrooms" were large out houses one for the boys and one for the girls. The parting words of the days' lesson the nun said "I don't know what I would do if somebody would write my name on a bathroom wall" ° For some unknown reason those words resonated in my mind. On my way, out to recess I grabbed a white chalk from the blackboard. I proceeded to the school outhouse and wrote the name of our teacher "sister m_____. In a very flowery cursive writing. We returned to the classroom and immediately one of the students announced "sister, sister your name is written on the boy's bathroom wall." Visibly disturbed she slammed the book on her desk and asked" "who did it?" The same guy that announced the presence of her name on the bathroom wall said, "it is a very nice penmanship it looks like Ben's handwriting" Bastard, I thought the evidence was overwhelmingly strong I did have an excellent hand writing. I was guilty and with great trepidation I awaited my punishment. I got a double whammy° I was ordered to go out to the hallway and there I was administered several whacks with a on inch wide leather strap on my open palm. A stinging punishment indeed, it took every ounce of courage to keep me from crying! On top of that I was deprived of recess for the entire month of April. And while everybody was enjoying recess each day I was given three by five yellow cards with ten long division problems. The redeeming benefit of my transgression was that it improved my mathematical skills.

There was one telephone in Park View. It was an old fashion phone which required asking the operator to connect you to a party. The lone phone resided in the town's grocery store. But even with this lack of modern communications news traveled fast. While in sixth grade, the nun required that we write our spelling words with definitions three times and turn them in as homework. I had a stroke of pomposity and completed my homework by writing the spelling words and definitions once and only once. Included at the bottom of the page was my sentiment expressed as follows∫ "writing the spelling words and definitions three times in nothing more than a waste of paper". I submitted my homework in midafternoon.

We usually sat down for dinner at about six o'clock. Before we started dinner my father hands me my spelling homework and in a very stern language he asks "What is the meaning of this?" Of course, I wondered how did this paper get to my Dad so quickly? There was no fax, no email, to this day I do not know how the nun got the paper to my dad. My response to his question was a wimpy excuse claiming I did not have enough paper. His advice was "when you need paper for school you come to me and don't write notes to your teacher." Besides my bout with a case mumps that was the highlight of my sixth-grade year.

CHAPTER 8

El dia De Santiago
The Role of religion

A gentle wind was blowing that early July evening causing a few tumbleweeds to glide across the highway. We could hear soft howling of the wind "winter is coming" my mother said. It was July 25th El dia de Santiago. St James is the Patron saint of Spain and most residents of Northern New Mexico trace their origins to early Spaniards that came to New Mexico in the 1500 and so Santiago day was revered as a special day in Park View.

The reverence for Santiago started in Spain during the period when Queen Isabella and King Ferdinand joined forces to expel all the Moors and Jews from Spain. The year 1492 which we learned in school was the year Columbus discovered America. Regretfully this same year a royal decree was issued ordering Jews and Muslims to choose baptism or exile!

The legend goes that Santiago the apostle that spread Christianity in Spain" appeared one night to the Commander of the Spanish Army. He instructed him to attack the Moors the following day. As the Spaniards engaged in battle the following day they saw St. James riding a white horse and waving a sword leading the Spaniards to a victorious defeat of the Moors.

I doubt that few of any of the residents of Park View knew of the Santiago Legend. However, that did not stop them from the tradition to make the 25th of July a day of celebration. Santiago day was a big feast day in the town of Park View my boyhood home. As a young boy I looked forward to this day. Relatives that had moved away to the cities such as Denver, Santa Fe, and Albuquerque returned to visit their respective families. We had many visitors and my mother cooked many delicious pies cakes and other goodies in anticipation of the big day.

Since it was a religious holiday the main activities were church related. The evening before the feast day we attended Vespers. This service consisted of singing special hymns and psalms followed by special prayers and ending with the benediction of the Blessed Sacrament. At the time, I did not really understand or appreciate the religious significance of the event but the whole family attended. Santiago Day started with a solemn mass. A solemn mass in those day was celebrated by three celebrants (priests). To young altar boy the mass was most impressive with three priests conducting interesting rituals. I remember the mass was a "high mass" much longer than the usual Sunday Mass. After the mass came the procession. The congregation lead by the three priests would walk in procession down the one street of the village singing the prayer Hail Mary. We always walked in the procession but I always wondered why most of the men would choose to stand on the side of the road and watch the people in the procession. The procession was led by men riding on beautiful horses that were decorated with colorful ribbons and bells strapped across the horse's chests. The back and forth prancing of these beautiful animals made the bells ring in a truly festive background sound as the congregation sang in Spanish....

"Dios te Salve Maria
Llena eres de gracia
El Senor es contigo y
Bendita tu eres entre
Todas las mujeres
Y bendito es el fruto
De tu vientre Jesus.

Santa Maria, madre de Dios
Ruego por nosotros pecadores
Ahora y el la hora del la
Muerte, Jesus Maria!

The ritual was simple yet solemn elegant and gave the day a true spiritual fulfillment. The day was more than visiting relatives and church activities. The community usually staged a parade that featured local beauties riding on a convertible or on the flatbed of an old chevy truck. The Native Americans for the nearby Jicarilla Reservation would perform their native dances and maybe the local band would play the favorite ranchera Mexican song.

At our house lunch after Mass was the festive meal of the day. My mother went all out° A beautifully prepared roast beef or maybe some delicious chickens mash potatoes fresh vegetables and of course those heavenly desserts. After that we would head to the carnival or the local rodeo.

For me it was primarily simply looking at the carnival booths. I don't remember ever having any money to spend on carnival gimmicks. Interestingly, being without money never seemed to bother me. I distinctly remember the time a friend of my dad" John Caranta an Italian gentlemen recognized me as Pablo's son and give me a fifty cent piece. Wow what a thrill that was. I so treasured the fifty cents that I could not bring myself to spend it on some carnival gadget or those delicious smelling hamburgers. I kept my four bits tightly held tight in my hand in my pocket. 41

Another afternoon attraction was the rodeo. The local cowboys would compete in various events such as calf roping steer riding and bare back bronc riding. None of the local cowboys were expert riders. This was one of two days in which this sport was practiced. It was fun to watch we got a big thrill by watching all these macho men bite the dust with amazing regularity.

Upon completion of the rodeo the next big event was horse racing. The racing track was an abandoned air landing strip. The owners of the race horses would parade the horses in front of the anxious crowd. Somehow the horse owners agreed to race their respective horses. I never understood how that came to happen. After the racing agreement the next order of business was to agree on the distance of the race. That settled the horse owners would pace out the distance. This pacing activity was witnessed with great anticipation by the entire crowd. Additionally, the crowd got fired up by betting with each other.

Once the finish line was established the crowd moved into position at the finish line so they would witness the winning horse. The other end of the track where the two race horses. I distinctly remember a tall black mare named Midnight. The owner/jockey of this magnificent animal was a gentleman about seventy-five years old. The jockeys usually raced bare back no saddles. To insure the safety of this older gentleman jockey he was strapped to the horse with a four-inch canvas belt. With his legs bent jockey style the attendants wrapped him securely with an impressive set of racing goggles he was now ready for the race!

Starting the race was always problematical. There were no starting gates. Ideally" the jockeys would walk the horses to the finish line and on cue the race would start. However, that seldom happened. The horse anticipating the race would get very nervous and difficult to control but after numerous false starts the race would start° By the time the races were over it was approaching sunset. We would head home" listening to the wind my mother would say "winter is coming". That night the community convened at Lito's Ballroom. An old dance hall with a unique architecture. A giant pillar in the center of the hall held up the roof. The crowd danced around the pillar all night. The end of the dance was signaled when the band played "Home Sweet Home" time to go home! Incidentally that was the only time I heard that tune°

CHAPTER 9

A brief New Mexico History

Most Anglo Saxon Americans view Hispanic people in this country as recent arrivals from Mexico and Central America. The fact is that Spaniards, my ancestors, arrived in the New World before the Pilgrims landed at Plymouth Rock in 1620.

In 1536 Cabeza de Vaca Estevan the Moor and others began rumors of the Seven Cities of Cibola as he and his Spanish soldiers explored the southwest in search for gold. During the 1500s and 1800s the southwest what is now Arizona Colorado New Mexico and Texas many Spaniard established villages and large ranches. The king of Spain granted hundreds of acres of land to the settlers in land grants called "Mercedes. "The land grant in Park View was known as the Tierra Amarilla Land Grant. To this day many residents of the area feel the land grant was taken from the illegally. These sentiments have contributed to feeling of mistrust between the Hispanic people and the Anglo population in the area. The following is a brief history of The Tierra Amarilla Land Grant. This brief history was Researched by Robert Torrez who served a State Historian for the State of New Mexico. Mr. Torrez was born and raised in my community of Park View later named Los Ojos. .

Courtesy of the State Records Center and Archives.
Reproducing prohibited without express permission from the State Records Center and Archives.
Tierra Amarilla Grant and Thomas B. Catron
By Robert Torrez

The history of the Tierra Amarilla Grant is relatively well known and will not be discussed here in detail. Suffice it to say that in 1832, the Mexican government made a community grant of that name to Manuel Martinez, his sons, and a number of individuals from the Abiquiu region. In 1856, however, Francisco Martinez, Manuel's son, applied to the Surveyor General for confirmation of the grant as a private grant. Through a series of machinations, we are now only beginning to understand, the United States Congress confirmed that and a number of individuals from the Abiquiu region. In 1856, however, Francisco Martinez, Manuel's son, applied to the Surveyor General for confirmation of the grant as a private grant. Through a series of machinations, we are now only beginning to understand, the United States Congress confirmed the grant as such in 1860.

It should be noted that the name of the grant does not historically refer to the present-day village of that name. Instead, it refers to the region encompassed by the Tierra Amarilla Land Grant and its original communities of Los Ojos, La Puente, Los Brazos, Ensenada, and Las Nutritas. Las Nutritas' name was changed to Tierra Amarilla when the Rio Arriba County seat was moved there in 1880. Sale of interests and speculation on the grant began almost immediately after it was confirmed by Congress. By 1880, Thomas B. Catron had purchased sufficient interests in the grant from Martinez heirs so that in February 1881, when the United States Congress issued a patent for the grant to Francisco Martinez, Catron himself signed the receipt. By 1883, Catron filed suit to quiet title to the grant, exempting only a few "informal conveyances of some very small pieces of land." These parcels, which have become known as the "Catron exclusions," were the donaciones, or allotments, made by Francisco Martinez to more than one hundred settlers of the grant. These were the same individuals to whom Martinez gave hijuelas, or deeds, which stipulated their rights to free use of the grant's common lands.

Even before Catron received quiet title to the grant, he had begun developing its vast natural resources. He leased right of way to the Denver and Rio Grande Railway, sold rights to the region's coal mines and massive pine forests, and leased its lush pastures to large cattle companies. During this period, however, there is little evidence Catron aggressively curtailed Tierra Amarilla's settlers from grazing their personal livestock on the traditional common lands of the grant. Introduction of the railroad and extensive lumbering operations in the region apparently brought prosperity to Tierra Amarilla during the 1880's and 1890's. As long as local residents had access to grazing for their small herds and flocks, the nuances of who retained legal ownership of common lands did not seem to be an important issue.

Interestingly, in northeast New Mexico at the time, the gorras blancas, or white caps, were waging a campaign of political activism and violence to protest the fencing of traditional grazing lands. The tranquility of Tierra Amarilla prompted pioneering archaeologist and historian, Adolph Bandelier, to comment about it. In 1891, Bandelier traveled through northern New Mexico and recorded the Tierra Amarilla grant's resources for Thomas Catron, who was desperately seeking a buyer for the heavily mortgaged property. Bandelier was clearly impressed by "Catron's grant" and in his journal, he describes it as "a most valuable piece of property, a little kingdom of its own." Then he added a statement clearly designed to assuage the concerns of potential buyers about whether the influence of the gorras blancas extended to Rio Arriba. "There is no trouble to be apprehended from the people [of Tierra Amarilla]," Bandelier noted, "unless there should be a leader."

However, this began to change after 1909, when Catron finally succeeded in selling the grant. When the Arlington Land Company obtained ownership, it continued the practice of selling timber and mineral rights to various companies. The company also sold large tracts of land to corporations and individual buyers, many of whom further subdivided the land. When these new owners began to fence off large portions of the grant, they initiated a process which began to severely restrict the access to pasture on which the settlers of the grant depended for their livelihood.

The residents' ability to access pasture for their livestock appears to be the principal reason why there is little documented evidence of resistance or protest to Catron's purchase and ownership of the Tierra Amarilla grant. In 1889, several residents of the grant filed a suit against Catron but did not ask for return of the grant or make access to land an issue. Instead, the plaintiffs cited the stipulations of the original grant and the hijuelas, which were issued to individuals by Francisco Martinez in the early 1860's, and sought a share of the proceeds Catron was receiving from leases and sale of timber and mineral rights. The few extant records of this case tell little beyond the fact of its dismissal in April 1892. Although there is little evidence that Catron moved aggressively against grant settlers who grazed their livestock, he occasionally took action to counteract perceived threats to his ownership. In 1892, he filed suit against Miguel Chavez and Pablo Rivas for allegedly pasturing their sheep on his property and sought a restraining order to prevent their further use of the land. Chavez and Rivas responded that while Catron may have been given patent to the Tierra Amarilla Grant, they were grazing their sheep by right of the grant made to Manuel Martinez by the Mexican government and the deeds, which allowed them "free and common" use of water, pasture, and other resources of the grant. They claimed to be doing nothing illegal and asked the court to force Catron to produce proof of his ownership. The suit lingered in District Court for nearly ten years and was finally dropped from the docket in 1902. The record shows Catron paid the court costs, which amounted to less than ten dollars for various filing fees.

So why did Catron go after Chavez and Rivas when he tended to leave everyone else alone? The case documentation provides few clues, but part of the answer may lie in the fact that Miguel Chavez was not your typical Tierra Amarilla settler. He was a wealthy.

There was also an element of political enmity between Catron and the principals in these suits. Chavez and Rivas' attorneys, Jacob H. Crist and N. B. Laughlin, were Catron's bitter political enemies and had represented the Tierra Amarilla settlers in the previously mentioned 1889 suit which had sought to force Catron to disclose and share the revenues he was receiving from the grant. Neither of these cases was resolved in court, and both were dropped for reasons not reflected in the documentation. It seems clear from this activity that many Tierra Amarilla residents were aware of Catron's ownership and exploitation of the grant. Adolph Bandelier's statement, which was quoted earlier, implies as much. He didn't say people were unaware, only that they apparently had no leadership which could galvanize protests or other such activity. Is this lack of leadership the principal reason why there is so little indication? of grass roots protest about what was happening to the grant? There is no doubt that in that age of robber barons and powerful patrones, the development of effective leadership among the settlers of the Tierra Amarilla could easily have been thwarted by the political and economic control exerted in Rio Arriba by a number of Catron's political allies. In Tierra Amarilla these would have included Thomas D. Burns, who had significant interests within the grant, and Wilmot E. Broad, Catron's agent for the grant.

It seems, however, that a principal factor in this process was Catron's apparent ability to placate local concerns with assurances that although he now owned the grant, nothing would change for the rank and file. What form these assurances took is a mystery, but every indication is that as long as Catron owned the grant local residents were not actively denied access to common lands. Evidence that Catron made such assurances surfaced in 1919, a decade after he sold the grant. That year, the first signs of protest in Tierra Amarilla finally made their way into the documentary record. We can only speculate why it took ten years after the sale of the grant for protests to galvanize and surface. The timing may have been a factor of how long it took the various new owners to fence off enough of the common lands to impact the settler's ability to graze their livestock. Large-scale fencing in the region had apparently begun in earnest soon after the grant was sold in 1909 and may have progressed significantly by the time the United States entered the Great War. It is probable that the war, and the subsequent enlistment of many of the region's young men in the armed forces, was enough of a distraction to delay an organized reaction to the fencing until after the war. In August 1919, a significant stretch of fence erected by George Becker and H. L. Hall near Ensenada, two miles north of Tierra Amarilla, was destroyed. El Nuevo Estado, the local newspaper, reported the damage had apparently been done by the same individuals who had previously left some warning notes signed "La Ley Secreta" and "La Mano Negra" at various locations. The newspaper does not elaborate on the locations or the contents of the notes, but this report is the earliest documented instance of such activity attributed to the infamous secret organization of the "black hand" in the Tierra Amarilla.

When Becker complained to Governor Octaviano Larrazolo, the Governor had the incidents investigated and stated his intention to mediate a solution between Becker and the residents of Ensenada. However, no meeting of conciliation ever took place, and it was speculated that Larrazolo had been pressured to change his mind. Further incidents occurred in 1924. For nearly the entire decade of the 1930s, there seems to have been no reported activities which can be clearly identified as related to land grant protest. Then suddenly, on the night of June 25, 1940, nearly twenty miles of "four strand barbed wire" was cut at several locations throughout the grant. Once again, George Becker's fences were targeted, although much of the destruction concentrated on new fences which had been erected near Chama and at Keeth A. Heron's property, west of the Chama River.

State Police Lieutenant J. P. Roach was sent to investigate this most recent outbreak. His report specifically attributed these activities to the "apparent revival of the Black Hand gang, commonly known as the Tierra Amarilla Organization." Lt. Roach, however, failed to identify any suspects and reported that he found "public sentiment as a whole is much in favor of the offenders." Lt. Roach concluded that subdivision and fencing of adjoining lands were "the basic cause for the present trouble." His report continued:

The people feel as though the land belongs to them, and should not be fenced. They are living under the illusion that years ago the Tierra Amarilla Grant was disposed of by the Grant owners to Col. Catron without the heir's or relatives consent. Colonel Catron, in turn, disposed of parts of the Grant to individuals with a verbal permit to them to use adjoining lands for their grazing and wood privileges (sic - emphasis added).

Once again, the issue of Catron's assurances raised its head. It had been more than thirty years since Catron had sold the grant in 1909 and a full generation since the first outbreak of fence cutting had occurred in 1919. Yet, the memory of Catron's long broken promises obviously lingered. As in all previous investigations, this 1940 incident produced no suspects. It also is the only time an official report specifically mentions the mano negra in association with, or being responsible for, this type of activity on the Tierra Amarilla Grant. Following the 1940 outbreak, national and international affairs once again seem to have interfered with further developments. After World War II, there appears to have been a lull in these activities except for a few incidents of burning and fence cutting that were reported in the 1950s and early 1960s. This restless slumber was broken on June 5, 1967, by the incident which has become known as the Tierra Amarilla Courthouse Raid.

SOURCES USED

Anselmo Arellano. "The Never-Ending land Grant Struggle." La Herencia del Norte (Summer 1996): 15-17 _____.
La Tierra Amarilla: The People of the Chama Valley. Tierra Amarilla: Chama Valley Public Schools, 1982.
Catron, Thomas vs Miguel Chavez and Pablo Rivas. Rio Arriba County Civil #490. Rio Arriba District Court Records, SRCA. Ebright, Malcolm.

The Tierra Amarilla Grant: A History of Chicanery. Santa Fe: Center for Land Grant Studies, 1980.

Gardner, Richard. !Grito! New York: The Bobbs Merrill Company, Inc., 1970.

Lange, Charles H., Carroll L. Riley and Elizabeth L. Riley. The Southwest Journals of Adolph F. Bandelier, 1889-1892.

Albuquerque: University of New Mexico Press, 1984. El Nuevo Estado, Tierra Amarilla, NM, August 11, 1918; April 26, 1920.

Roach, Lt. J. P., Report: June 5-25, 1940. John E. Miles Official Governor's Papers, Correspondence, State Police, 1939-1942. SRCA. Seth, Theodore, Manuel Romero, Juan Trujillo et al. --vs- Thomas B. Catron. Rio Arriba County Civil #490. Rio Arriba District Court Records, SRCA.

Torrez, Robert J. "El Bornes: La Tierra Amarilla and T.D. Burns." New Mexico Historical Review 56:2 (April 1981): 161 175. _____.

"The Tierra Amarilla Land Grant: A Case Study in the Editing of Land Grant Documents. " Southwest Heritage (Fall 1983 / Winter 1984): 2 16. Westfall, Victor. Thomas Benton Catron and His Era. Tucson: University of Arizona Press, 1973.

• 2004-2014 New Mexico State Record Center and Archives

It was not until 1807 that Zebulon Pike led the first Anglo-American expedition to New Mexico. Anglo Americans were indeed late comers to New Mexico° Instead of giving you a lesson in New Mexico History the following timeline will give you a a quick view of the history of the State of New Mexico and illustrates the presence of Hispanic people in the entire southwest long before the pilgrims set foot on Plymouth Rock.

New Mexico Historical Timeline

1200s - 1500s® Pueblo Indians established villages along the Rio Grande and its tributaries
1536® Cabeza de Vaca Estevan the Moor and others began rumors of the Seven Cities of Cibola Gold®

1540® Francisco Vasquez de Coronado while searching for that gold discovered the Grand Canyon

1598® Juan de Onate established San Juan de los Caballeros as the capital 35 miles north of the city of Santa Fe.

1600s

1600® San Gabriel founded as the second capital

1601® Colonists deserted San Gabriel

1609® Governor Pedro de Peralta established new capital at Santa Fe

1626® Spanish Inquisition established

1641® Governor Luis de Rosas assassinated

1680® Pueblo Indians forced colonists and Spaniards to retreat to Mexico

1694® Captain Francisco Lorenzo De Casados born in Cadiz Spain his wife and son arrive at Santa Fe NM. He was banished from Mexico City to Santa Fe for a period of ten years

1700s - 1800s

1706® Villa de Albuquerque founded

1743® French trappers reached Santa Fe

1807® Zebulon Pike led first Anglo-American expedition to New Mexico

1821® Mexico declared independence from Spain[a] Santa Fe Trail opened

1828® Gold discovered in Ortiz Mountains

1837® Governor Albino Perez and top officials assassinated in revolt against Mexican taxation

1846® Mexican-American War began[a] Stephen Watts Kearny annexed New Mexico to U. S.

1848® Mexican-American War ended[a] Treaty of Guadalupe Hidalgo signed

1850® New Mexico designated a territory[a] denied statehood

1854® Gadsden Purchase added 45˝000 square miles to territory

1861® Confederates invaded New Mexico[a] Territory lost northern-most section[a] Territories of Arizona and Colorado created

1863-1864® The Long Walk - Navajos and Apaches relocated to Bosque Redondo

1868® Navajos and Apaches return to homelands

1878® Railroad arrived

1881® Billy the Kid shot

1886® Geronimo surrenders[a] Indian uprisings ceased

1898® Thomas Alva Edison produced first motion picture in New Mexico

1900s

1909® Northern New Mexico Spanish American School is established.

1910® New Mexico Constitution drafted

1912® New Mexico became 47th state

1916® Francisco Pancho Villa attacked Columbus New Mexico

1920® Women won the right to vote

1922® Oil discovered on Navajo Reservation

1942® New Mexico soldiers forced to endure World War II Bataan Death March

1945® World's first atomic bomb detonated at Trinity bomb site southern New Mexico

1947® Alleged crash of UFO near Roswell

1948® Native Americans won right to vote in elections

1950® Uranium discovered

1980® Deadliest prison riot in U. S. occurred at New Mexico State Penitentiary

1982® Space shuttle Columbia landed at Holloman Air Force Base

1998® New Mexico celebrated cuarto centenario 400th anniversary of its founding

2000s

2000® Valles Caldera National Preserve established

2005® 11. 65• of state's employment was derived directly or indirectly from military spending

2008® New Mexico had highest poverty rate in US

2009® Death penalty abolished

2010® Runway opened at world's first spaceport in New Mexico

2010® Governor Richardson announced he would not pardon Billy the Kid
2011® Wildfire forced officials to close Los Alamos National Laboratory voluntary evacuation issued for residents

The Spanish Inquisition was initiated by King Ferdinand and Queen Isabela in 1492. Jews and Muslims were banished from Spain or if they chose to remain the would have to convert to Catholicism. Those who converted but still retained their Jewish beliefs were called Crypto-Jews or conversos It is believed that many Spaniards that settled in Northern New Mexico were "Crypto- Jews" that fled the tortures induced by the Spanish inquisitors. Older residents remember customs such as lighting candles on Friday nights the day before the Sabbath. a Jewish tradition. The new techniques of tracing genealogies have further re-enforced the theory that many Northern New Mexico residents are descendants of Crypto-Jews that fled from Spain in the during the 1500s through the 1800s. The rules of the inquisition was revoked by the Spanish government in the middle of the 20th century.

The Casados Family arrives in Park View, New Mexico

By 1938 we were a family of five. I had three older brothers and an older sister. Since I was born in 1936 I have no memory of La Jara Ranch. I vaguely remember our first home in Park View. It was quite close to the Brazos River a small river that flowed generously during spring and early summer. During the late summer its level of water was greatly reduced since most of its water was diverted for the irrigation of the hay fields in the valley.

Our home was a crude structure. It was made of split Juniper logs placed in a vertical position and then plastered with mud. I believe it had a dirt floor I do not recall a linoleum and of course there was no carpet. If there was a carpet it would have been homemade. The women in those days would create strips of cloth from rags and then weave them into long 36 inch strips. These would then be sewed together to create a "rag carpet". The house had no electricity or plumbing. Lighting was provided by small kerosene lamps. The bath room was an outhouse with the standard Sears or Montgomery Catalog. There was a basin for washing hands and face. A bath occurred once a week it usually was a Saturday night affair. Water was heated outside and brought in in pails. Baths usually took place in the kitchen. Notwithstanding the absence of modern conveniences, we had a very happy life. We always had plenty to eat. My mother was a magnificent cook. We were always dressed appropriately for the weather and my father would never allow us to walk around barefooted. We always wore shoes.

Two years after our arrival to Park View we moved to a more suitable home which me father bought from my aunt and uncle. The house consisted of three rooms two bedrooms and the kitchen and it did have an unfinished attic. My parents fixed an area in the attic and set up a bedroom for me and my three brothers. We slept in the attic during the summer months. My father feared a fire so there was never heat in the attic. In the summer was all slept downstairs in one bedroom.

The town its people and it customs and tradition. Park View in my youth was a small community. The area had several small communities. Park View was the focal point primarily because it was the parent parish. All three parish priests lived in the Rectory of St Joseph Catholic Church. Tierra Amarilla three miles away was the Rio Arriba County seat. The presence of the court house gave that community some status. Ensenada directly east of Park View La Puente to the west and Chama, a bigger town was due north.

From age two until I was seventeen years old I lived in the warm embrace of these communities populated by Hispanic people. My mother's relatives lived nearby so it was great to grow up with uncles and aunts and numerous cousins.

I was about seven years old when world war II started. My uncle Eddie, my mother youngest brother, was drafted into the service. My mother was heartbroken when he left he was her favorite brother and the youngest in her family. Fortunately, he never faced frontline duty. He was trained as a barber and spent his entire four-year army career cutting hair in a London Army Hospital.

I distinctly remember our neighbor's son going away to the service. The only commercial transportation was a bus. It delivered the mail in the morning and at four o'clock it returned south to Santa Fe. We gathered at the roadside where "Pilo" would board the bus and be off to his days as a soldier. He was wearing a cowboy hat a black leather jacket a maroon western style shirt with pearl buttons levi pants and cowboy boots. "After many tearful hugs and good byes, he waved goodbye and boarded the bus. We never saw him again. He was killed in action in Iwo Jima. He was an only son. When word was received of his death the church bells tolled. The bells tolled many times during the war years many young men from the surrounding villages died in action.

Fortunately, my father was never drafted. He was in his late thirties probably too old to be drafted and by then our family numbered seven children. Two sisters followed my birth one in 1938 and one in 1941 Another sister came in 1946 and at the age of 45 my mother gave birth to my youngest brother in 1952.

Life in our ranch was an ongoing series of activities. My father pursued a variety of money making activities. We raised hogs sheep and planted fields to harvest wheat and barley. Harvest time was an exciting time. First the wheat and barely had to be cut and bound into bundles with a machine called a wheat binder. We would stack the bundles in a vertical position in groups of three to five bundles. The excitement for us came on thrashing day. Mr. Rhodes owned a large threshing machine and my father hired him and his machine to come to our house to thresh our wheat and barley crop.

This was a big day that required close coordination. In the early morning, I would hear the put put of the tractor towing this giant monster gray thrashing machine that looked like a folder dinosaur. A site was selected and the machine was carefully backed into a level position. The threshing machine was powered by the tractor' engine and a giant belt attached to the tractors pulley. As the machine came to life the various parts began to shake some move vertically and horizontally. The bundles of grain were feed through a giant opening at one end of the thresher as the golden crests of grain moved through the various screens what to me appears a miraculous process grains of wheat or barely would stream down a metal pipe into gunny sacks. The opposite end of the machine was a giant pipe about fifteen feet long that spewed out the straws defrocked of the crests of grain.

Another important aspect of threshing day was the various wagons pulled by horses that brought the bundles of grain from the fields. Each wagon was manned by at least three men. Once the thresher as started it had to be fed continuously. So, having the necessary wagons and man power was most essential. All this activity on made for an exciting day for a young boy°

During the summer my older brother, Ted and I were in charge of taking care of a small herd of sheep, we had in our ranch. After breakfast, he and I would push the herd out to the river bottom for pasturing the herd. The Brazos River and the Chama River converged below our house. This required for us to move the herd across one of the rivers.

My parents had a very strict rule about our shoes. My father never allowed us to walk around barefooted. By the same token, we were responsible for taking very good care of our shoes. That included a cardinal rule "never get your shoes wet°" Since we were on foot my brother and I had to wade across the river. My brother Ted suggested we take off our shoes and tie them around our neck. He then reconsidered. The water was above our knees and the current was a bit swift he feared the current would knock me down and my shoes would end up getting wet. He did not seem to be overly concerned about me drowning his goal was to prevent my shoes from getting wet.

He suggested that instead of me walking with my shoes tied around my neck he would throw the shoes across the river one shoe at a time. He took one shoe and hurled it safely to a dry spot across the river. He took my second shoe and hurled it across. This time the shoe floated momentarily in midair and fell on the river current floated for a moment or two and then disappeared in the waters of the Chama River never to be seen again. How would I explain the loss of my shoe to my parents?

We came home quite late that day. We slept in the attic during the summer months. I place my remaining shoe on the outside staircase. The next morning, I announced one of my shoes was gone. My cousin had a pretty hound dog named Rusty. He had a habit of caring things, off never to be found again. I used poor Rusty to explain the disappearance of my shoe° My parents accepted my story°

My little sister, Josephine was born in 1938. She was a beautiful young girl. I vividly remember her gorgeous fair skin and light brown almost blond hair. My parents detected that as a child she would tire easily. The local doctor diagnosed her as having a leaking heart valve. I those days open heart surgery was an unknown. She died in April of 1948. I was in the back of house chopping wood. It was my responsibility to provide enough chopped wood that would last 24 hours. My father was not home probably out in the fields. My brothers and sisters were in school. I have no idea why I was home on this school day. My sister died at about three o'clock. While I was chopping wood I heard loud music playing above our house. I was startled. I ran into the house and asked my mother "what is that loud music over the top of the house" She said to me "Josephine just died in my arms go get your father°" I have never been able to explain what I plainly heard as loud music emanating from the top of our house. My father was most intolerant of noise and so we did have a radio in our house so the music did not originate from a radio While I cannot explain it I choose to call it a spiritual experience. The untimely death of my sister was a difficult time for my family. My father was inconsolable and my mother was devastated by the loss of her dear daughter. Because of her condition she was everybody's favorite. My oldest sister had a very difficult time resulting in a near nervous breakdown. With the burial of my sister we sadly faced the longest and saddest summer of 1948.

When I entered seventh grade in 1949 our Saint Joseph public school was now Saint Joseph Parochial School. We had of own vs Board of Education. When Brown vs the BD of Education was passed, that prohibited nuns from teaching in public schools. This caused great turmoil in our community. Nuns had been the local educators since the school was established. So now it was up to the community to provide the financial resources for the operation of a parochial school

St. Joseph Parochial Schoo
Park View,New Mexicol.

The first order of business was to get a commitment from the Franciscan order of nuns to provide the nuns needed to operate the schools. After numerous bingos and cake raffles enough money was raised to send the parish priest to Indianapolis, Indiana the religious home of the nuns. He drove to Indianapolis. Why it was necessary to make a road trip to Indianapolis is unknown and was never explained. Thinking back, it appears the a letter of request would have served the purpose. However, the trip was successful and the nuns would remain in our community as teachers of the new parochial school. Raising money to operate the school now became a concern of the parents of school children. Each weekend a bingo was standard practice. The prizes were never money. Most of the prizes were donated by local businesses. They were usually cans of food or garden tools such as shovels axes and hammers. I distinctly remember winning at bingo. my prize was an ax handle no ax just the handle. I attended our parochial school through the ninth grade. After my class completed the ninth grade the school never offered classes beyond the eighth grade. Many years later the community was unable to support the school. Sadly, the school closed and that was the end of a sound educational elementary school program and religious instruction. A few years later the church council decided that rather than seek funds to maintain the building they decided to destroy the building and bulldoze down the hill. I was gone from the community when this happened. Had I been there I would have fought to preserve the building. After all the school building which included the residence for the nuns was built entirely by donated labor from community volunteers. It was indeed a sad day when I learned the building had been demolished. The demolition of the school building was to me a sign that the community was no longer the cohesive community that worked together to solve problems. The social matrix of my little town was beginning to unravel.

Tierra Amarilla New Mexico is the county seat of Rio Arriba County. I attended High School at the Tierra Amarilla High School about three miles from my home in Park View. It was a county school housed in an ugly building that looked like a storage facilities for potatoes. Nothing spectacular except that we had a staff of very dedicated teachers. The curriculum was limited. There were no science labs no home economics kitchens and a very limited library. Overhead projectors or movie projectors were non existent. We had textbooks and chalk boards and as I said before a faculty of very dedicated teachers.

Nothing very exciting happened during my high school days. I entered High School in the tenth grade. I took the bus every morning at about eight forty. My dad had a small dairy and every morning I got up at about five o'clock to milk about 15 cows. This was a chore that I performed every single day. No holidays. Those cows had to be milked every morning and every night. In the evening, I got home from school at about 4:45. I would have a small snack and off I went to the dairy to milk the cows. Economically it was great for my family. It provided a pay check twice a month. A steady income was not common in a ranch environment. We received money in the fall with the sale of cattle or sale of lambs the rest of the year was quite lean financially. My father was a real go getter. Most homes burned wood for heating and for cooking. We had a truck so during the winter months my father would cut two loads of wood each day. In those days, he sold a load of wood for eight dollars. On the weekends we headed for the woods early. My father would throw some apples in the glove compartment and of we went. We had no power tools. A crosscut saw and axes is all we had. On Saturday, we would deliver about four loads of wood to local people. It was a simple way to earn extra cash.

A neighbor once acquired a chain saw. I was most impressed. I wanted my father to see a chain saw in action. I invited my neighbor to join us in woods one Saturday morning, to demonstrate the wonderful power of this technology. We arrived at the woods and proceed to attempt to start the chain saw. We pulled and pulled the crank rope many times. The darn chain saw just would not start. I was most disappointed. My father said, "bring down the crosscut" The was the end of my attempt to introduce new technology to our wood cutting business.

I played football and basketball at 140 pounds I was not much of a threat on the football field but I enjoyed the game. The same in basketball at five feet six inches I played the game barely. Athletics were not my forte but I did excel in the classroom. I was the valedictorian of my 1954 graduating class.

The saddest day of my life came in January of my senior year of 1954. At about 3:00 AM my father came up to my room and announced my mother was bleeding excessively. He sent me to my Uncle home in search of a remedy to stop the bleeding. I do not recall the name of the remedy, unfortunately he did not have "it". That same night I helped place my mother in the back of the local doctor's Jeep wagon. There was no ambulance. The doctor was driving and he and my father went off to the Hospital in Santa Fe NM one hundred miles away.

I was the oldest sibling at the time living at home I was a senior in High School. My oldest brother had returned from the service and had moved his family to Henderson Nevada. He worked for Stauffer Chemical Company. The next brother, Ross was serving in the army stationed in Germany. My third brother was also living in Henderson Nevada and my older sister was attending a business college in Pueblo" Colorado. Besides me living at home was my 13-year-old younger sister another little sister age 9 and my baby brother 16 months old.

On this particular day after my usual chore of milking the cows I boarded the bus and went to school. I distinctly remember sitting in my English class and I looked out the window and saw my Uncle Julian walking towards the school. He was my mother's older brother. He had no reason to visit the school so immediately I surmised bad news. Sure enough, a pounding knock at the classroom door sounded most alarming I came out. He put his arms around me held me and told me my mother had passed way that morning in the hospital. It was in the middle of January.

My mind was a total blank° I could not imagine my mother gone forever. I have no memory of how we got home. My uncle did not have a vehicle so somehow, we got home on this very cold winter day.

Later that day my Father asked me to call my brother who was stationed in Germany. I was a senior in High School. I had never used a telephone placing a call to Germany seemed a most formidable task. I walked to the general story where the only phone existed. I remember picking up the ear piece and cranked the phone. The operator came on. I related to her my mission of informing my brother of our mother' demise. She connected me to the Red Cross. I gave the location of my brother's army station. I learned the he got the message four or five days later. I guess I had accomplished my goal.

I might add, the winters in Park View are extremely cold. That year had been a very cold and snowy winter one could see only about eight inches of a five foot fence posts. We had had a lot of snow that winter.

When the mortuary brought my mother's body she was laid out in the living room of our house. My bedroom was directly above the living room and I must admit it gave me an eerie feeling to know that my mother lay in a lifeless state on the floor below. The traditional rituals for the dead in Park View were pretty standard. The village had a designated group of men that prayed the rosary with the family relatives and friends. In those days, Los Penitents were part of the wake. This is a religious organization that dates back to early Spain. During the Lenten period, it was said The Penetentes would scourge themselves. Supposedly, a re-enactment of Jesus being scourged prior to his crucifixion. The group sang some rather haunting chants. These chants I hastened to add echoed in my brain and added to the sadness of my mother passing. The next day my mother's body was taken to St. Joseph Catholic Church for a mass for the dead. After mass, a large entourage of cars with many people headed to the cemetery.

We buried my mother on a bright and cold January morning and we returned home. All the visitors were now gone and I remember we all sat silently in the kitchen. The silence was broken only by the cracking of the ceiling as house warmed up after a long winter night. I kept asking myself "How are we going to manage without my mother?"

My two brothers returned to Nevada and my older sister returned to college in Pueblo Colorado. Ross, one of my brothers was in Germany he came home in April of that year. I resumed my daily chores milking cows and going to school. It was a tough semester. Coming home after school was a most trying experience. My younger sister who was in the eighth grade assumed the household duties. Poor girl she was very young to assume all the household duties. My father would tote my baby brother around as he did the ranch work. In order for my little brother to ride safely on the tractor my father who was most ingenious removed the tractor fender and on its place" bolted a twenty-five-gallon barrel. The barrel was the ideal size my little brother stood in the barrel with his chest and head protruding above the rim of the barrel. It was an unique child safety device for use on our Farmall H tractor.

I stayed focused on my school work and helping my sister around the house. Of course I still had the duty of milking our cows that continued seven days a week. The spring of 1954 was very sad with trying days. Somehow, we managed to survive the loss of my mother was extremely hard and difficult on my father. As I mentioned before my father was basically uneducated. He could read and write in Spanish but he relied on my mother for clarity in the English-speaking world. Each evening at the dinner table my father would weep uncontrollably and we all sat in silence and quietly weeping inside.

I wanted to attend the Junior-Senior prom. I was hesitant simply because I did not own a suit. My uncle, one of my father's brother in one of his rare visits had left an old blue suit at our house that fit me quite nicely. Even though its flared pant style was 30 years old. I had worn it to the prom the year before so I decided I would ignore the style and go for it. Lucky for me my brother had come home to get married. Detecting my wardrobe dilemma, he and his fiancé went to Espanola and bought me a beautiful beige suit with a single bottom coat. I was most appreciative pleased and I might add very stylish. I was the president of the senior class and I invited a girl whom I admired tremendously as my date. Her name was Geraldine Esquibel, she accepted. It was a memorable date. I never dated while in High School this was only my second date I did go to the prom during my Junior year. Going to the prom in my senior year was indeed a significant event in my young life. I borrowed my Uncle's pickup truck washed it an laid an Indian blanket on the seat. I was ready for an exciting evening I seventeen years old. May 25th, 1954 was my high school graduation date. I was the valedictorian of the class. I was happy to graduate however, with my mother's recent death it was not a very happy occasion. She had always admired and was very proud of the academic accomplishments. I had always had very good grades in school. Her absence on this day of my academic milestone caused me to miss my mother even more.

I was now ready to face the adult world. As valedictorian, I received a tuition scholarship to Highlands University a teacher training university located in Las Vegas" New Mexico. I had visited the University during a field trip. I was not impressed with the campus or facilities. I had a totally different mental image of what a University should be. Highlands was not it. I never acknowledged the scholarship I had made up my mind to go join my best friend, Manuel G. Martinez, and go to New Mexico State University a place I had never visited. One of my father's friend was a county commissioner. A position of some influence in our rural county. He arranged a job for me as a summer recreation director at the local high school. I had no idea what a recreation director position entailed. Actually, I had never had a paying job. My summers had always been ranch work" irrigating cutting hay baling hay and bucking bales and of course milking cows. About 20 young boys showed up for my recreation activity. In the morning while the temperatures were cool I would organize a game of softball game. The kids went home for lunch and would return in the afternoon. It was hot so I would then organize a basketball game in the gymnasium.

It was a pleasant summer and I was able to earn a few dollars. My salary was §15o. 00 a month however a condition of my employment was that I would give his son half of my earnings. So, I ended up with a monthly take home pay of about §70. 00 a month. The job lasted two months by the time I left home for college I managed to save §75. 00. This constituted my entire "college fund". I knew my father did not have the resources to pay for my college education and I did not expect him to do so. I was confident I would be able to find a job to pay for my tuition books and living expenses. I had graduated from High School but besides a high school diploma I had a Ph. D in Naiveté.

I am off to college . When I arrived at New Mexico State University to start my college career I had $77.00 in my pocket. Not enough money to even pay for one semester of tuition. In my heart, I knew I could somehow find work to pay my educational expenses. I worked at mowing lawns, a house cleaner for two older ladies, a waiter in a restaurant, dish washer, and finally a cook at the University canteen. All these odd jobs contributed to a meager existence. My father did not have the means to support me or my educational costs. Through diligent effort I was able to pay for my living and educational expenses. The key word here is diligence, discipline and desire to succeed.

I enrolled at New Mexico College of A and M now known as New Mexico State, in September 0f 1954. In those days college tuition at New Mexico A &M was §50. 00 a semester with an additional student fee of §15. 00 which allowed students to attend athletic events and other recreational campus activities. I signed up for a room in decrepit WW II barracks for §40. 00 a semester. The accommodations in these barracks were quite primitive.

Bare concrete floors one heater shared by two rooms and wooden barn doors with padlocks. This housing accommodations were indeed primitive and cheap. After two years the University condemned the structures and I moved to the Freshmen dorm the oldest dormitory on campus. An adobe built structure that cost §54. 00 a semester. A great deal for a poor student.

Books were not very expensive in those days but these meager costs when set next to my college fund of $70. 00 it did not take a financial genius to conclude I was in financially deep yogurt. To the credit of the University they had a benevolent credit policy. I was able to register with a minimum down payment. However, on the first day of classes I was flat broke. I bought a box of cereal and powdered milk and lived on that for several days. I reported to the job placement office and pleaded for a job. Nothing was available. Finally, after three weeks had elapsed the lady at the placement office found me a house cleaning job. Two elderly ladies lived at the edge of the campus. On one afternoon a week I would clean their house. They were very picky. They did not wash dishes for the entire week. They had old magazines and newspapers stacked two feet high in the living room. When I arrived, they presented me with rubber gloves. I was to wash the dishes in boiling water. They paid me 75 cents an hour and deducted fifteen minutes of my pay whenever I went to the bathroom. The three dollars a week sustained me food wise for a few weeks.

I had a difficult time with my cash flow. The second semester of my sophomore year I was completely broke and no possible employment. I enrolled into school. When I could not come up with some cash I was politely told I could not continue to attend classes. I packed up my meager belongs and went home. I was down but not out. I was determined to return to the university.

Upon my return I *m*anaged to get employed at the University cafeteria as the designated assistant to the pot washer. A real low level position, the advantage of working in the food service was being in close proximity of food. Even though it was against the rule to eat while working I became an expert at sliding a whole banana down my throat is a single fast motion. I moved up the kitchen "management organization" from assistant pot washer to a baker's aid then as head breakfast cook and eventually as night manager and cook for the University canteen. This was a job where I worked from 4 PM till 11:00 PM. Even though this was a most demanding work schedule at 95 cents hour I ate regularly. This job provided me the financial resources for surviving college poverty. They paid monthly and after they deducted my meal ticket I usually "took home" about §15. 00 for monthly cash flow.

I was undecided about my career goals. Career guidance did not exist in my little High School. I registered with an undeclared major. This gave me the option of choosing whatever course, I wished to take. I aspired of being a doctor so I finally declared a major in Biology. My college days were uneventful. My recreation consisted of attending football and basketball games. I did make a few trips to Juarez Mexico. I attended a few night clubs and had a few Margaritas. We would bring back a bottle of Rum which in those days sold for about 90 cents for a liter of rum. A real bargain. After four and a half years of financial struggles I graduated in June of 1959. I graduated with a B. S. a Major in Biology and a teaching certificate. I did not tell a soul I was graduating. After the graduation ceremony my girlfriend, Erlinda Hovey and a couple of friends came by and I believe we went out for lunch. The next day a packed my few belongings and went home expecting to be drafted into the military.

CHAPTER 10

I am a college graduate

The summer of 1939 I was helping my father move a herd of sheep to the San Juan mountains north of Park View and near the Colorado state border. It was a trek of about twenty miles. We started out very early in the morning and by mid afternoon we passed the herd through downtown main street of Chama NM.

A mile passed downtown Chama we stopped for a break it was a sunny hot June day. It was a beautiful setting. The 1200 sheep grazed lazily in a green meadow next to the Chama River. The mountains lay to north and beautiful cumulus clouds lingered overhead. The cool temperature was in the low 80's with very low humidity. It was indeed, a magnificent and beautiful day in Northern New Mexico.

My father's friend who owned the Frontier Bar in Park View joined us while we were resting. He brought out a six pack of Coors beer and he and my father proceeded to enjoy what appeared to me as a refreshing and delightful drink. I was 21 years old but in the eyes of my father and his buddy I was just a kid. They never offered me a beer. Being the respectful son that I was I did not have the guts to ask them for a beer. All my life I have had a problem asking for anything that day was no different. I sat in silence and accepted the fact that I really did not need the beer and I would never ask for one. A strange thought entered my mind. Here I was with a B. S Degree and herding sheep I wondered about my future.

I did not seek employment upon graduation. I had taken ROTC during my freshman and sophomore years. I enrolled in advanced ROTC with the understanding that upon graduation I would serve three years of active duty in the Air Force, with a commission of a second lieutenant. However, before my first semester of advanced ROTC started I was informed that I would have to serve five years of active duty. At the time, I was not inclined to spend that much time in the service. The good Air Force Captain Nolan informed me that if I dropped out of ROTC he would arrange for me to be drafted upon my graduation. With that threat over my head I was not motivated to seek employment after my college graduation.

My brother in law, Frank Valdez, was working with a road construction company working on a road leading to the Jicarilla Indian Reservation near Park View. He got me a job as a laborer. A few days after my start day the foreman approached me and said "I hear you have a college degree." I said, "yes I do". He threw a roll of blueprints and said "you are in charge of building the cattle guards". Realizing that my college education provided no training in building cattle guards I asked" can I get some help from the working crew?" Absolutely he said. I then proceeded to recruit some of the more mature laborers that I knew and had some carpentry experience. I succeeded in placing the cattle guards with the help of very experienced fellow workers.

While installing a cattle guard a big yellow Cadillac drove up. A distinguished white haired gentleman stepped out and announced, "I am looking for Ben Casados" I stepped forward and inquired "what can I do for you Sir?" He said, "I understand you are a certified science teacher and I need a Science Teacher at El Rito Normal School?" I said "I am but I anticipate getting drafted into the army any day so I am not really available." He informed me that the president of his board of regents was also president of the local selective service board and had enough influence to get me deferred from military service. I was never anxious to join the service. I accepted his offer as a science teacher with minimum discussion I never even inquired about the salary I later learned I had agreed to work for $3,600.00a year.

Faculty at Northern New Mexico Normal School
Left to right Silas Lopez, Math, Ruben Lucero Coach, Ben Casados,
Science, Amado Valdez, Business

Employed as a science instructor at Northern New Mexico Normal School

The Spanish American Normal School at El Rito NM is a unique educational institution in Northern New Mexico. This boarding school was established in 1909 with an endowment established by Colonel Venseslao Jaramillo. The

71

New Mexico Territorial Legislature determined that a facility was needed in Northern New Mexico with the primary purpose was the training of teachers for the Hispanic population of Northern New Mexico. When New Mexico was admitted into the union in 1912 the State Constitution Article 12 Section 11 designated the Spanish American Normal School as one of the educational institutions which would be supported by the state. The "Normal" at that time provided both secondary and post-secondary educational programs. Teaching the physical sciences at the "Normal" school was a challenging experience. The professor. Dr. Douglas that directed Practice Teaching at New Mexico State was a real professional. While doing my practice teaching at Las Cruces High school he observed my classes he always had tons of advice and suggestions on the art of teaching.

I prepared diligently for my classes. While I felt confident of my content area I felt somewhat inexperienced about life. I was raised on a ranch seldom visited a city. I spent four and a half years at the university town of Las Cruces and traveled to nearby El Paso and Juarez Mexico a few times. I considered myself a true hayseed and had difficulty relating science to everyday life. I was always in a preparation mode and tried my best to be an excellent teacher. To this day, I consider teaching the hardest and most taxing work I have of ever done. What made teaching so fatiguing to me was the multiple requirements on a person. The job requires you to be "on" all day. By "on" I mean you performing before an audience that may or my not want to be there. You have to speak clearly and convincingly you have to be cognizant of each student in the class. Are you reaching them" are you maintaining their interest? Are your students learning? These questions drive your performance in the classroom and thus at the end of the day you are a very tired and a drained "puppy".

The Principal, Mr. Melvin Cordova, was an excellent educational leader. I walked into his office one day seeking advice for a discipline solution. I was having some trouble with one of my students. I walked in and recited a litany of complaints about this one student. He listened to me intently and then quietly he pulled up a large sheet of blank white paper.

He proceeded to draw a small black circle on the white sheet. He said to me "Ben you are focusing on the black circle which are the negative aspects of this student's behavior. Let's look at this large white area which constitutes the whole person this student represents. He then guided our discussion with strategies on how to address the student's behavior with emphasis on the positive aspects of this student's personality.

It was a valuable lesson for an inexperienced teacher on how to cope with student behavior. I have never forgotten this discussion and to this day I try not to focus on the black dots of human behavior but rather the "white area" of human personalities.

President Kennedy was assassinated while I was on the faculty at El Rito. It was a sad day for the nation the staff, and the student body. The nation had never experienced a presidential assassination and we all felt a sudden emptiness. President Kennedy was a young president and young people identified with his youth and forward looking agenda. After all he was the one that set the moon landing as a national goal.

On that day, the student body and faculty assembled in the school gymnasium. For some strange reason the principal of the school asked me to make memorial speech. Of course I was totally unprepared. Whatever I said was totally extemporaneous. I remember speaking of his bravery in World War II his early political history his dedication to family and his efforts on civil rights. I spoke for about fifteen minutes and remember ending my little speech quoting President Kennedy: "

"And so, my fellow Americans, ask not what your country can do for you—ask what can you do for your country. ...Finally, whether you are citizens of America or citizens of the world ask of us the high

standards of strength and sacrifice which we ask of you.... With a good conscious as our only sure reward, with history the final judge of deeds, let us go forth to lead the land we love, asking His blessing and His help but knowing that here on earth God's work must truly be our own."

It was a day like we had never experienced in our lives. The audience responded silently as we all emerged from the assembly to face a different country. Being a teacher was a most rewarding experience. I was 21 years old and I consider it part of my growing up years. Since it was a boarding school it had a real feeling of family. The student came from rural and city environments. I felt very close to my students and some of them to this day remain very close to me. I have been involved in the school alumni organization and continue to maintain contact with my former students. This includes, Theresa Lobato Wells. Tally Wolfe, Leo Valdez, and Roberta Orona Cordova and other students. That fall I was admitted to enroll for graduate work at Michigan State University. I left my students and friends in El Rito with a heavy heart.

CHAPTER 11

I am accepted to Graduate School at Michigan State University

Going to Michigan State University was indeed a unique adventure. I had never been away from New Mexico except for a few visits to El Paso which was thirty miles south of New Mexico State University. And now I was heading for the Midwest and a Big Ten University. I was married to Erlinda Hovey, in June of 1961. My wife and I headed for Michigan in late August of 1962 in a 1955 Ford Crown Victoria.

The first night we drove from El Rito to Wichita Kansas. My wife Erlinda, had a sister that lived in Wichita. We spent a couple of days and then proceeded east. Somewhere along the way we stopped for the night. When I went to check in the clerk inquired of my ancestry. When I queried him as to the reason for his question his aggressiveness subsided and he proceeded to provide a room for me and my wife. Remember, this was 1962 before Civil Rights legislation had not been enacted and since I did not appear to be lily white, the clerk could have easily refused to honor our room request. Sadly, had that happened in those day I had little or no power to demand accommodations. Thanks to the efforts of Lyndon Johnson Civil Rights became the law of the land in 1964.

We arrived at Lansing, Michigan, the home of Michigan State University and proceeded with the ritual of finding our apartment at the University married housing complex known as Spartan Village. We moved into our one bedroom apartment. It was more than adequate and considerably more modern that our apartment in El Rito, NM.

I had struggled with poverty throughout my undergraduate studies. Going to school under the auspices of The National Science Foundation NSF was a real luxury. NSF paid for my travel to Michigan paid my tuition gave me a book allowance and a monthly salary that was more than my teaching salary of $3,600 a year. I was in great financial shape and I would be getting masters degree thanks to the financial assistance of NSF and the tremendous diligence on my academic pursuits.

The middle sixties were a wakeup call for American education in the field of science and mathematics. The educational community had designed various curriculum versions of physics chemistry biology and mathematics. The goal of the NSF was to improve the academic background of science teachers. My undergraduate major was biology. Michigan State per NSF policy was to enhance my background in Math Physics and Geology.

Lacking undergraduate study in these areas and being thrown into graduate level courses presented to say the least a significant academic challenge. We were a group of forty teachers from all over the United States. I was the only representative from New Mexico. I felt I carried the reputation of the state as far as my academic accomplishment. The entire group was dedicated to hard work regardless of undergraduate limitations.

Since I did not have any financial worries I approached my studies like an eight to five job. Each day I would go to the campus at eight in the morning and return home at five. Any time I was not in class I spent studying. Each night and every weekend were likewise dedicated to study study study.

Two very significant events occurred at Michigan State. In March of 1963 my daughter Michelle was born at Sparrow Hospital on a very rainy day in March the 19, 1963. She was a tiny beautiful baby with enchanting eyes, she brought us tremendous joy. In June of that year I completed the academic requirements for a Master's degree. With those accomplishments my wife and I, with our new baby, Michelle we headed back to El Rito"NM.

While in Michigan a NASA representative approached me on the possibility of joining NASA educational program. The agency in its effort to fulfill the requirements of the Space Act to inform and educate the public of NASA's programs of space exploration and the results of their scientific investigations. NASA was particularly interested in my academic background in Biology, Math, Physics and Geology. Of course, these areas were most relevant to Space Science. Additionally, NASA had an international cooperation program that involved tracking stations in Mexico and South American. . Thus, they were most interested in my fluent Spanish and my teaching experience.

I was flattered to be considered for this prestigious position. It involved traveling throughout the country and the Spanish speaking world of Mexico South America and Puerto Rico. The El Rito Administration had granted me a leave of absence to pursue a Masters Degree. I had made a commitment to return to my teaching position upon completion of my graduate studies. With that commitment, I did not feel I could accept the NASA position. So, I returned to El Rito and back to my teaching job. I pursued my teaching duties with great diligence. My enhanced science background gave me additional confidence and a broader prospective of strategies for teaching science. I continued to strive to be an excellent teacher to engage my students and give them a greater appreciation for the field of science.

While teaching I always felt that I needed to broaden my life experiences if I was to continue to improve my excellence in teaching. Completing an advanced degree certainly, enhanced my ability to teach. However. I was always looking for opportunities outside the education world.

The Federal Department of Health Education Welfare had a position in Phoenix Arizona as an education specialist. I applied for the position. After an interview in Albuquerque I was hired to start my job in June of 1964.

The job was not particularly challenging. It paid a bit more that my teaching job but the work was not rocket science. It involved visiting medical doctor's office and informing them of the latest drugs in treating venereal disease. Venereal disease was on the rise as a result of soldiers returning from Vietnam with drug resistant venereal diseases. Additionally, another element of the job required tracking individuals who had been diagnosed with venereal disease and interview these patients about their sexual contacts. Once contacts were identified my job was to make sure they were brought in for treatment.

The work was certainly mundane and the disease was not a topic for party conversation. The people and doctors at the clinic where I worked were most friendly and dedicated. It appeared at the time I was launching a new career in health education. I was mildly enthused°

CHAPTER 12

NASA A New Beginning

At the end of the summer in 1964, I had a pleasant surprise. I was contacted by NASA, they were still interested in hiring me as a Space Science Specialist. I flew to Washington DC for an interview. This was the first time as a passenger in an airplane. I boarded the TWA plane in Phoenix in the late evening and proceeded to act like a seasoned traveler. I took my seat and waited with great anticipation for the lift off. The plane took off on a hot Phoenix evening and as the plane lifted off the ground and while in low flight plane dipped down caused by the hot thermals. I perceived as a dangerous and treacherous maneuver causing me to hang on tightly with white knuckles to the armrests. The stewardess looked at me and casually commented "first time up huh" That ended my seasoned traveler demeanor as I glanced out the window anticipating my first visit to the world's seat of power Washington D. C. our nations' capital.

I arrived early in the morning at what is now Reagan Washington Airport. I changed into my interview suit and proceeded by taxi to the interview site. At ten in the morning I was interviewed by two NASA gentlemen and asked to return in the afternoon for a third interview. Since I had never been to Washington I welcomed the opportunity to walk around and do a little sight-seeing. It was late June and the summer temperature in D. C. was beastly hot and humid. I walked around for about two hours and then detected considerable crotch discomfort. I had never experience hot humid weather. In my brief period of exploration I developed a major heat rash with all associated discomforts. I returned for my last interview. I thought it went well but I detected one of the NASA men was not fond of Hispanic candidates.

He questioned me on my ability to speak English to a large audience. I was not hired. I returned to Phoenix with a severe heat rash and no NASA job.

I must admit I was surprised of the results. My interaction with a NASA representative at Michigan State had been most favorable. He wanted to hire me on the spot. A month after my Washington interview I received a call from the NASA Education Officer in Santa Monica California. He was the education officer for NASA Western Operations office. He asked me to come for an interview in Santa Monica. I reminded him that I had flown to Washington at my own expense with negative results. He insisted I get to Santa Monica he was most anxious to meet me. I could not afford another plane fare so I boarded the Greyhound Bus to Los Angeles. It dropped me of in the center of down town Los Angeles. I walked out of the depot and spotted a bus showing a Santa Monica destination. I boarded it asked the bus driver if he went near 150 West Pico Boulevard in Santa Monica. To my most pleasant surprise he said that address is one of my stops in Santa Monica. What luck for a hayseed that had never been to Los Angeles. The bus dropped me off at the front door of NASA Western Operations Office.

The NASA gentleman in Santa Monica was most gracious he was anxious to hire me and wondered why Washington had rejected me. He called the Washington Office and after some loud exchanges he asked if I could start working on September 1, 1964. I returned to Phoenix with great joy announced my new job to my wife. I resigned my old job and moved my family to the Los Angeles area. Little did I know I was embarking in a most exciting employment adventure.

I reported to NASA headquarters in Washington D. C on September of 1964 for three weeks of intensive training on all NASA programs. My new job involved making assembly stage presentations to elementary and secondary schools, university audiences as well as civic organizations. It required intimate knowledge of all application programs scientific programs and manned spaceflight programs. At this time, NASA was well-funded and had a large number of research programs including application programs such as weather satellites communication satellites and scientific programs such as the orbiting geophysical observatories orbiting solar observatories orbiting astronomical observatories and of course the manned spaceflight programs which included the Mercury Gemini and Apollo programs.

Thirty men were selected to educate the populace of the United States on NASA programs and the benefits derived from these programs. Remember this was the mid 1960s. There was no Internet no social media and mass communication relied on printed media a few TV channels and radio.

The selected candidates were paired into a team of two lecturers and assigned to the various NASA centers nationwide. I was teamed up with a retired Air Force colonel and assigned to the Manned Spacecraft Center in Houston Texas. My program coordinator was located at the Manned Spacecraft Center in Houston. After three weeks of intensive training I was assigned to work in the schools in Oklahoma City where my partner picked me up at the airport. Our assignment was to present Space Science Lectures to High Schools middle schools elementary schools in the State of Oklahoma. Additionally, we were scheduled to make presentations to the Lions Club and other civic organizations. Our first stop was John F Kennedy High School in Oklahoma City.

It was at John F. Kennedy high school that I first encountered and experienced the sting of discrimination. The Colonel and I arrived at the school and were cordially met by the high school principal. He guided us to a beautiful auditorium where we were to make the presentation to the entire student body. While we were setting up the models and equipment to be used during the presentation the principal ordered one of the student helpers to go and get some coffee. The student left and quickly arrived with two cups of coffee one for my partner the Colonel and one for the principal. The Colonel inquired what about the coffee for Mr. Casados? The principal said "oh we did not get one for him". The Colonel said "Mr Casados is making the presentation this morning. " I suspect the principal assumed I was the Hispanic flunky to be treated as such. The embarrassed principal now offered me his cup of coffee. To which I responded "no thank you I believe you need the coffee more than I".

My presentation to the student body was enthusiastically received with a standing ovation. I felt great. The principal behavior I never forgot but I quickly realized I was no longer in New Mexico where Hispanics were the majority. I was in the real world where I was a minority and I had to endure whatever came my way because of my cultural background. I had always strived for excellence this incident motivated my pursuit for excellence even more.

Being assigned to the Houston Manned Spacecraft Center was not what I expected. I had moved my family to the Los Angeles area so being assigned to the mid-west was not an ideal situation. My immediate goal was to somehow change my assignment to the west coast. Eventually I was assigned to NASA Ames Research Center in Mountain View California. After a year I was finally assigned to the NASA Santa Monica Office which was closer to my home in Huntington Beach California.

The NASA STAGE PRESENTATION

The presentation included excellent scale models of launch vehicles" communication satellites weather satellites and various observatory spacecraft models. The model of the Saturn V launch used for the Apollo flights to the moon was most impressive. The model stood about four feet tall and truly conveyed the magnitude of the Apollo mission to the moon Besides the scale models was had a device that illustrated the concept of telemetry receiving date for a spacecraft in orbit.

Our presentation discussed basic laws of physics as they related to rocket propulsion and attitude control system for spacecraft inflight control. Rocket propulsion was dramatically illustrated by placing a sponge in a beaker saturated with alcohol. We would ignite the alcohol and then after a dramatic discussion and demonstration of the cold liquid oxygen we would pour the liquid oxygen into the flaming alcohol. The result was a loud roar and flame leaping from the innocuous beaker. This demonstration clearly explained the basic principles of combustion occurring in rocket engines when rocket fuels were combined with pure oxygen.

For historical context, we would relate stories of a fabled Whan Who a famous Chinese rocketeer that supposedly tried to launch fellow Chinese colleagues into orbit by strapping him to a rocking chair with one hundred Chinese rockets attached to the chair and ignited simultaneously. Kids got a big kick from this story°

Making these presentations required considerable depth of knowledge on all NASA programs and public speaking ability and the creative use of language that made complex science topics engaging understandable and interesting.

My work with NASA occurred during the sixties. The voyage to the moon was a prime project at NASA. Several preliminary projects related to the manned lunar landing was initiated.

The Ranger project managed by the Jet Propulsion Laboratory in Pasadena involved sending a spacecraft to the moon that prior to its crash landing would photograph the surface of the moon. After several attempts, Ranger 7 successfully give us the first close-up pictures of the surface of the moon. Concurrent to the Ranger projects the Lunar Orbiter project. A spacecraft was place in orbit around the moon. This spacecraft while orbiting the moon sent back excellent high resolution images of the surface of the moon.

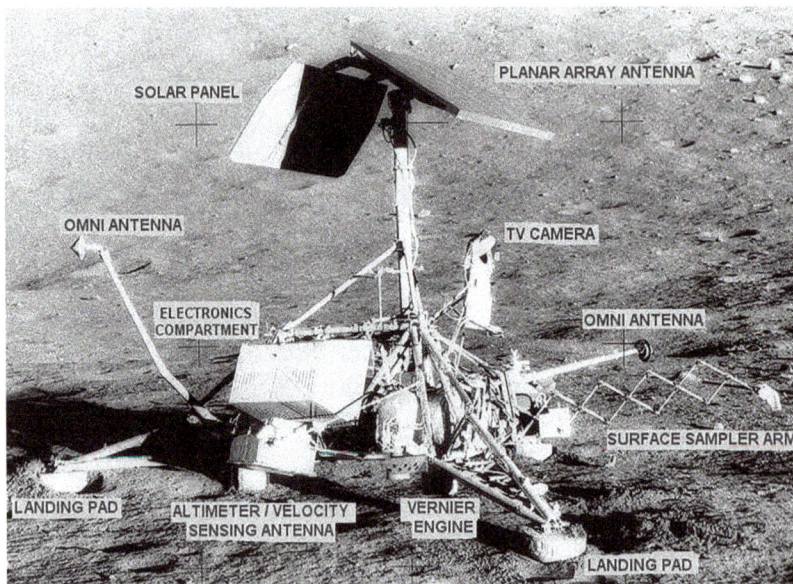

The **Surveyor program** was a NASA program that, from June 1966 through January 1968, sent seven robotic spacecraft to the surface of the Moon. Its primary goal was to demonstrate the feasibility of soft landings on the Moon. The Surveyor craft were the first American spacecraft to achieve soft landing on an extraterrestrial body. The missions called for the craft to travel directly to the Moon on an impact trajectory, a journey that lasted 63 to 65 hours, and ended with a deceleration of just over three minutes to a soft landing.[1]

The program was implemented by NASA's Jet Propulsion Laboratory (JPL) to prepare for the Apollo program, and started in 1960. JPL selected Hughes Aircraft in 1961 to develop the spacecraft system.[1] The total cost of the Surveyor program was officially $469 million. Five of the Surveyor craft successfully soft-landed on the Moon, including the first one. The other two failed: Surveyor 2 crashed at high velocity after a failed mid-course correction, and Surveyor 4 lost contact (possibly exploding) 2.5 minutes before its scheduled touch-down.

All seven spacecraft are still on the Moon; none of the missions included returning them to Earth. Some parts of Surveyor 3 were returned to Earth by the crew of Apollo 12, which landed near it in 1969. The camera from this craft is on display at the National Air and Space Museum in Washington, A third project called Surveyor was designed to soft land on the surface of the moon. Once on the moon the Surveyor would send thousands of pictures of the moon surface surrounding the Surveyor. A critical tend conducted by surveyor was a sco0p the probed the surface of the moon and collected samples for on board chemical analysis of the surface lunar soil. The Surveyor spacecraft where a tremendous engineering and scientific success. The success of soft landing an unmanned spacecraft on the moon was a giant step in fulfilling our national of landing a man on the moon° Witnessing the successful launch of Apollo Eleven the first successful landing by humans on the moon.

I was fortunate enough to be assigned to work at the VIP site on the Kennedy Space Center during the launch of the Saturn V Rocket of Apollo 11 the first mission to land on the moon.

Author describing the model of the Saturn V moon rocket

It was a warm sunny morning at the Kennedy Space Center Launch Complex number 39. The countdown had started early in the morning as the Astronauts Neil Armstrong" Edwin Aldrin and Michael Collins had an early morning breakfast and were transported to Complex 39 to enter the Command Module positioned at the top of the 36-story high launch vehicle.

On this warm and sunny July morning, the VIP site was crowded with celebrities from all over the world. I had the honor of meeting former President Lyndon Johnson a tall distinguished gentleman that championed civil rights and was a great supporter of NASA space exploration programs. The King of Spain was in attendance many senators and famous people from the entertainment world. My role was simply as an information source to those in attendance.

We all waited with great anticipatory fervor as the countdown proceeded to 10-9-8- 7-6-5-4-3-2-1- ignition started° I saw the flame of five giant rocket engines erupt at the base of the rocket...the sound reached my ears seconds later since the VIP site was about a mile away the roar was unbelievable° I had previously observed a test firing of one F-1 engine is the Santa Susana mountains in California it was most impressive. Five engines firing at the same time was most astonishing. The giant rocket stood motionless for a microsecond and the slowly it moved upward rising on a column of fire. The monstrous white rocket slowly cleared the launch tower as it rose slowly almost reluctantly into the earth's blue sky.

The sound of the five giant F-1 rocket engines roared popped and created a pulsing vibration in your lungs. The crowd applauded briefly and then silently watched as three human at the top of a column of fire were being accelerated toward a point in space where they would be inserted into an earth orbit one hundred miles above the earth at an orbital velocity of 18"000 miles per hour. We observed the flight of the rocket until it disappeared from sight. . We all silently walked away from the site pondering the dangers of the flight and anticipating the landing on the moon that would occur on July 20, 1969. It was indeed one of the most dramatic events in my life.

The NASA Space Science education was a huge success. Thousands of students and teachers received excellent science instruction and motivation to pursue their studies in science and mathematics. Personally, I had the opportunity to meet some very dedicated teachers and school administrators. I also made some troubling observations. I was amazed of the limited science background elementary school teachers possessed. During the time for 1964 to 1972 that I was making presentations in schools throughout the western states my observations of teachers' low competency in science and math were consistent. The problem seemed to persist in urban schools as well as rural schools.

People question why America's student rank so low when compared with other students worldwide and we usually come up with a variety of excuses. One of the common reasons given is class size if too big. When I was in elementary school each classroom had two grades. The total number of students was usually about 40 students. Another reason commonly offered is that some students come from economically deprived homes. I have never seen any data that state that students from poor family have limited learning capabilities. While I was in elementary school the whole school came from economically depressed conditions. Not enough technology in the classrooms our total technology consisted of paper pencil chalkboard and "black board" we did not have an overhead projector. Each student had his or her own textbooks° It appears state funding could provide this minimum requirement. I will admit the student coming to school Hungary could impede their learning but surly that is a small minority. All of these factors probably do contribute to poor student performance. In my own experience, I did not find these factors as obstacles to learning. However, perhaps a major contributing reason this educational deficiency may be the quality of preparation teachers get in our colleges and universities. I will not go into analyzing the college curriculum for training teachers. During the days when I was giving presentations to students of Space Science I visited many classrooms and spoke with hundreds of teachers I found teachers poorly prepared to teach science and mathematics. The educational community has been discussing ways and strategies for evaluating teachers. Most teachers are very dedicated individuals. Perhaps it is time to review and evaluate the curricula and methodology that colleges and universities offer to train today's classroom teachers. It may be time to require for elementary and middle school teachers to enroll in college courses that give them a greater depth of content in the areas of science and mathematics. Having a better and broader background in a curriculum area tends to give a teacher greater confidence in their teaching strategies and ultimately makes a better teacher.

Tour of Puerto Rico

Being fluent in Spanish presented me with interesting opportunities for work assignments and travel while working as a space science lecturer. One of my assignments where my Spanish played a role was a trip to Puerto Rico. I conducted a lecture series are the University of Puerto Rico for a group of teachers from the Puerto Rico Schools. It was my first trip to Puerto Rico and it exposed me to the island culture.

Getting to Puerto Rico was quite adventure. NASA arranged for my vehicle which was loaded with spacecraft models and other teaching aids to be flown to Ramey Air Force Base in the Island of Puerto Rico. I drove the vehicle to Patrick Air Force Base and waited for the plane that would transport the vehicle. And old C-119 came landed at the base flown by a National Guard crew. The crew was anticipating flying some exotic spacecraft to Ramey Air Force base. They were quite disappointed when they were informed their payload was a Chevy Van with spacecraft models. We loaded the van on the plane. There was no room for passengers so, I sat on the van's driver seat and fly to Puerto Rico.

We landed quite uneventfully on the landing strip at Ramey Air Force Base. The plane taxied to the far end of the tarmac. There we unloaded the vehicle. The crew fired the engines of the C_119 and took off back to Florida. I got into the vehicle and proceeded to drive it toward the airport terminal. Quickly I was stopped by flashing red light and questioned. "Where did you come from?" To which I responded "Patrick Air Force Base, Florida "They inquired "in this vehicle?" I explained I had been flown by a National Guard plane that had taken off . The base was in some kind of alert status due to some unrest in one of the Caribbean Islands. Seeing a van on the runway truly raised their concerns. After some discussion with NASA officials in Washington DC verifying my mission I was allowed to proceed to the University of Puerto Rico in San Juan, where I was to conduct Teacher workshops on Space Science.

On another occasion, I returned to Puerto Rico was for the purpose of serving as the science commentator on a Television program on Skylab. I brought to the Kennedy Space Center a television crew to videotape some footage related to Skylab. Skylab was a prototype space station. The third stage of the Apollo Saturn V rocket was modified with life support systems as living quarters for astronauts.

Skylab was launched on May 14, 1973 and placed into orbit 146 miles above the earth. It orbital speed was about 4. 8 miles per second. Its scientific objective was to study the effects on the human body of long duration space flights study the earth from an orbital observation site study of the sun and a variety of experiments related to it weightless environment.

Skylab was occupied by three different crews. It remained in orbit until July 11th 1979. The last crew shut down all systems and left the craft. When it orbital speed deteriorated it re-entered the atmosphere and scattered debris over the Indian Ocean and sparsely populated area of Western Australia.

Our three one hour television programs were enthusiastically received by the people in Puerto Rico and certainly enhance their knowledge of NASA manned spaceflight programs.

It was always a pleasure to work with the people of Puerto Rico. The Puerto Rican cuisine was always delight It was my first exposure to tostones deep fried plankton and other delectable items. Listening to a musical instrument unique to the island was the Cuatro which means four but it actually has five double strings. It makes a delightful sound somewhat like a Mandolin. I made several trips and conducted teacher workshops. I always found the teachers eager learners and ready to incorporate space sciences across the curriculum in Puerto Rico Schools.

Assignment South America

During the month of January, in 1968 I was assigned to a lecture tour in the schools in the State of Utah. It was a cold winter day in January when I got a call from NASA Headquarter in Washington. I was told to report to Washington NASA Headquarters and informed that I was being assigned to work in South America.

Washington was experiencing a horrible snow storm and traffic was barely moving. My first order of business was to obtain a passport. I had never been out of the county except for a few trips to border towns in Mexico which in those days did not require a passport. I obtained a passport and managed through the snow and taxi to visit the embassies of Peru, Chile and Argentina to obtain visas since I would be traveling in those countries. After a week of briefing from NASA and the Department of State on the "dos" and "don'ts" while traveling in this country, I flew from DC straight to Lima Peru. After a lengthy flight, I arrived in Lima. It was the middle of Summer.

My assignment in Lima was to report to the Instituto Geofisico who had a contract with NASA to operate a satellite tracking station in Peru. In those days, we needed tracking stations in South America to track polar orbiting satellites. My initial task was to conduct a space science teacher workshop the Catholic University in Lima" Peru.

During the time I was in Peru, NASA had successfully soft landed the Surveyor spacecraft on the surface of the moon. This spacecraft provided the first close-up pictures of the moon. Additionally, the craft tested nature of the lunar surface and confirmed that it would be safe for a manned landing on the surface of the moon. The subject of Space Science was quite foreign to the teachers in attendance however they were most enthusiastic to learn about the upcoming voyage by American astronauts to the moon. We discussed the role the country of Peru was playing in the space program. The Instituto Geofisico Del Peru was very much involved in tracking the Polar Orbiting Geophysical Observatory POGO, the Orbiting Solar Observatory, OSO, and other spacecraft functioning in polar orbits.

Since I had never been to Peru I took some time to explore the city of Lima. The history of Lima, the capital of Peru, began with its foundation by Francisco Pizarro on January 18, 1535. The city was established on the valley of the Rímac River in an area populated by the Ychsma polity. It became the capital of the Vice Royalty of Peru and site of a Real Audiencia in 1543. In the 17th century, the city prospered as the center of an extensive trade network despite damage from earthquakes and the threat of pirates. However, prosperity came to an end in the 18th century due to an economic downturn and the Bourbon Reforms.

Lima is a charming city with beautiful old building and wonderful art museums and impressive churches. The population in Lima is an interesting ethnic mix. I suspect there is heavy Inca heritage mixed Spanish ancestors. Additionally, at some time there was a heavy influx of Japanese into Peru. It was surprised to hear many Peruvian that looked Asian and were fluent in Spanish. In recent time one of Peru's president was of Japanese ancestry. Which perhaps also accounts for the Peruvian cuisine being influenced by Japanese cooking.

After I completed my assignment of presenting teacher workshops in Lima I started preparations to head south the Buenos Aires Argentina. The first order of business was to get the NASA vehicle trip worthy for a very long road trip. The vehicle was in bad shape. The drive shaft was broken it needed a new clutch. Apparently, it had been driven into the ground and the parked. It took about two weeks to get it fixed and about $3000.00 dollars. I convinced my engineering assistant to make the trip with. The trip seemed treacherous over rural areas of southern Peru and some pretty bad gravel roads. We started out early February day. Our intended first stop was to be the City of Arequipa. A small city located at the base of volcano called Misty. It was not a smooth ride. As I mentioned this was rural Peru. The service stations were not readily available. Gasoline was available from roadside vendors that sold gasoline in ten-gallon milk cans. What was no obvious to this marketing scheme was the gas contained considerable amounts of water. After "gassing up" we headed down the road observing the barren desert country side. All of sudden the vehicle started missing and hissing. My partner instantly diagnosed the problem. "Damn" he said, "they sold us watered gas!" Being a Peruvian, he was familiar with the practice of roadside gasoline sales. We were driving a somewhat old vehicle, one that had sediment bowls. We could see the sediment bowl was full of water. We were out in the middle of nowhere in the vast desert of Peru. We proceeded to remove the sediment bowl and empty the water. This enabled us to drive for another few miles. The sediment bowl filled with water and the vehicle stopped. We performed this sediment bowl removal until we reached the City of Arequipa. The we arranged to have the gas tank drained and filled it up with real gasoline.

The following day we traveled south towards Chile. The gravel road was rough and meandered sometimes along the beach and up to a low plateau with magnificent views of the Pacific Ocean to the west and the Andes Mountains to the east. We heard a loud bang and we knew we had a flat of some kind. We had a flat about a hundred miles south of Lima, So, at this point we did not have a spare tire, An oversight I should have anticipated the need for a spare tire and bought one. The only solution was to fix the tire. We did not have tools for fixing flats so we removed the tire and I flagged a truck that give me a ride to the small city of Tacna. The driver dropped me off at what appeared to be s service station. I rolled my flat tire into the tiny service station and asked if they would fix the tire. The owner politely said they did not fix tires and showed a small room with tools to fix the tire. He said I could fix the tire myself and I was welcome to use the tools. After a few hours of struggle, I was able to dismantle the tire and patch the inner tube and reassemble the tire back to a working condition. It was late in the evening so I inquired about a place to spend the night. Within in walking distance was a small motel. I rented a room which was very small about six feet by ten feet. It had a small bed, a small table and no bathroom. It was fine I was very tired and needed a safe place to sleep. I had a small breakfast and bought some bread and fruit to take to my traveling companion which I had left in the NASA vehicle up the road about thirty miles.

I walked and rolled the tire back to the main highway. A large truck with wine barrels were rolling down the highway. I flagged it, they stopped helped me load my tire and we headed North to the site where I had left the NASA vehicle and my traveling companion who had been waiting and guarding the vehicle for a day and a night. We installed the tire and continued our southern trek toward the Chilean border.

Crossing the border into Chile was not an easy task. All kinds of bureaucratic obstacles were encountered. For openers, the vehicle was owned by the U. S. Government on top of that it was loaded with spacecraft models and electronic equipment. The documents that had been provided by the Peruvian Auto Club did not satisfy the border patrol. I learned border patrol officials have omnipotent power to prevent crossing the border. Once such a decision to prevent passage is made it appears that no earthy power can override the hold decision. I was persistent in describing my educational mission and after two days we were allowed to proceed south. Our next destination was Santiago, Chile the capital of the county of Chile. Along the way, we spent a night in Vina Del Mar a beautiful seaside city on the on the beach of the pacific and near Valparaiso. From there we drove into the Capital city of Santiago.

At this point after many unanticipated expenses I was out of money! I related my situation to NASA headquarters. The proceeded to move money from the US to Chile. For some reason in those days money going to an individual in Chile had to be routed through the bank of Canada. Naturally that caused considerable delay. My Peruvian traveling companion decided we would be tourists until the money arrived. Santiago. Chile is a wonderful city and wonderful summer weather. With the Andes Mountains to the east the views of the city are magnificent. We proceeded to visit several historic land and architectural landmarks as well as several art museums with wonderful pieces of art.

The Chilean cuisine was most delightful. Since the city is so close to the Pacific Ocean the seafood and fish goes directly from the fisherman to the restaurants of the city. We also, discovered that Peruvian ceviche was as good in Chile as the one in Peru. It was outstanding!

When I was informed, the money was at the Bank of Canada, I picked up the money and headed east towards the Argentine border at the top of the Andes Mountains. We slowly made our way up the western slope of the Andes Mountains. We drove through a small town called Los Andes. The main industry in this small town appeared to be car radiator repair shops Driving up the Andes is a real challenge, especially for old cars. We drove cautiously and arrived at the border in midafternoon. I reported to the border patrol office for border clearance.

I was informed that the paperwork to allow me to bring a vehicle into Argentina had not arrived at the border. The auto club in Lima, Peru had assured me that the documents would be sent to Buenos Aires and from there wired to the border entrance at the top of the Andes. I was further informed that the documents had not arrived. The delay was caused by a Telecommunication's Strike in Buenos Aires. So, there I was stuck on top of the Andes! We had no idea when the paperwork would arrive. That night we slept in the vehicle. Lucky for me I still had my long winter over coat. Even though it was the middle of summer, in South America, at those elevations the nights got very chilly! The next morning a Border Patrol came by our vehicle and offered us some Mate a traditional Argentine caffeinated hot beverage, drank in the mornings in Argentina. As we were sipping our Mate with an interesting metal straw device. A gentleman approached our vehicle. He introduced himself and asked of our vehicle had been inspected. I informed him we were waiting for documentation from Buenos Aires and yes, our vehicle had been inspected. A few minutes later he returned with a small blue Pan Am bag. He said, " put this in your vehicle and let me see if I can get you passed the border." Later he returned accompanied with a Gendarme, an Argentine soldier. The soldier instructed me that he would accompany me to Mendoza the first city from the border in Argentina. The gentleman who arranged this for me was from Chile and he too was on his way to Buenos Aires. He asked to check into the Hotel Cervantes once I got to Mendoza and he would make contact with me there.

So, in the company of this Argentine soldier and his rifle we headed down the mountain to the city of Mendoza . I turned the vehicle to the Argentine customs office and proceeded to the Hotel Cervantes. It was a charming old hotel with a very polite staff. The custom's people introduced to the clerk as the "man from NASA" and provided me with a gorgeous hotel room.

About an hour later I heard a knock at my door. My Chilean friend had come to pick up his little blue bag. "Where is my bag" he inquired. I said, "here it is and by the way what's in it?" He zipped it open. The bag was full of American dollars of various denominations. I thought I have just smuggled money illegally into Argentina! It turned out this gentleman had a tire recapping business and was on a material shopping trip to Buenos Aires. He said the dollar value allow him to deal more effectively and get more and better products using dollars rather than using Chilean money. For all intends and purposes my traveling companion and I were stranded in Mendoza. He offered us a ride. That evening we dined together and enjoyed both the Argentine cuisine and several bottles of wine. The next morning, we headed east across the pampas, toward our destination, the city of Buenos Aires.

Buenos Aires is a fabulous city, considered the Paris of South America. It is a coastal city located on the eastern coast along the Atlantic Ocean. It was the middle of winter and after a month of traveling on the rode I was happy to be settled into a hotel. After the day of rest I reported to officials at the Argentine Space agency. The first order of business was of course to retrieve the vehicle from the customs office in Mendoza. A young man was assigned to retrieve it. Armed with appropriate documentation he succeeded in bringing the vehicle to Buenos Aires in two days. This young man was later assigned to be my driver while I was in the country,

My mission In Argentina was to train a person to make presentations about NASA programs on space exploration and the cooperative role that the government of Argentina was playing. A young engineer was selected. He was somewhat familiar with NASA programs, since he worked the Argentine Space Commission. I spent about two weeks training not so much on the content of the presentation but on public speaking strategies using spacecraft models and other electronic equipment. He was a most enthusiastic candidate and after a few dry runs with friendly audiences he was ready to go on the road.

During my stay in Buenos Aires I became quite friendly with my assigned driver. His family had a summer home somewhere south of the city. He invited me to spend the weekend at this summer home. The family picked me up at my hotel in a very old " "Diamond T" dump truck. The entire family was on board.

It was an extended family which included uncles, cousins and their children. I piled in the back and we headed out to the Argentine country side. It was a wonderful weekend. I had been away from my family for about two months and Argentine family warmly embraced my presence. They fed me generously with the local cuisine and excellent Argentine wine. Additionally, they had horses and I had the opportunity to ride in the local scenic area. After a wonderful weekend, we piled back into the old Diamond T and headed back to the city.

The people at the Space commission we wonderful and cordial hosts. On two occasions I was invited to dinner at their homes. I was aware that lunch is the main meal of the day. Lunch is thoroughly enjoyed by the locals, and it is a very large meal. Dinner on the other hand is a very light meal and served quite late at night. One night I requested one of my hosts to take me out to some night life. I was particularly interested in observing the Tango. The Tango originated in Argentina and for many years was considered to be a low brow dance. When it caught fire in France the Tango became s socially acceptable dance style. I had a few lessons on how to dance the tango. It was much more fun to watch it that my clumsy attempt to do the tango. I will admit however, that I enjoyed the proximity of my beautiful dancing instructor!

After closing the details of my mission with the Argentine Space Commission I and reported to the U.S. Ambassador. Upon I arrival, I had reported to him verifying my mission and identifying the agency with which I was to work. Consistent with proper protocol I gave the Ambassador a briefing of my completed work with the Argentine Space Commission. We exchanged pleasantries and I bade him farewell; my mission in Argentina was done. The next day I boarded Aerolineas Argentina and headed to Washington D.C. for my final report to NASA Headquarters and my next lecturing assignment.

Hawaii the Land of Waves, Balmy Winds and Sweet Smelling Leis

Upon my return from South America I was assigned to conduct an Aerospace Science Education Teacher Workshop at the University of Hawaii. I had been gone from home from home for three months and I was glad to be home with my family. My youngest daughter at first did not recognize me, that didn't make me feel very good. I decided that I would include my family in my next lecturing tour in Hawaii.

My wife, Erlinda, arranged to have an apartment in Hawaii available for our arrival. It was a very nice apartment located near the Ala Moana shopping center. The apartment belonged to an air force colonel who had been given a foreign assignment. It was fully furnished and so, we moved in with minimum complications. A wonderful Japanese restaurant called the Pagoda was close by. We dined there frequently and my two young daughters learned to enjoyed the Japanese cuisine.

Upon completion of my teacher workshop I was given a lecture itinerary for auditorium presentation to Hawaii schools on the island of Oahu, Maui, the big Island of Hawaii and Lanai. This lecture tour provided an opportunity for me to visit the Hawaiian islands. I discovered some interesting aspects about island students and island schools. To begin with schools seemed to be operated in a more relaxed mode. Discipline was not as rigid and other mainland schools that I had visited. I was introduced to a student audience in one of the high schools where the principal was unable to quiet the audience down to a level that I could proceed with my presentation. I made a gallant effort to get the students attention. My efforts were all in vain, the students had no interest in the topic of space exploration. I saw no benefit in my efforts and so I walked off the stage. The principal was most apologetic and asked me to resume my lecture. I politely refused packed up my props and departed.

Thinking back, I now realize that the subject of space exploration was indeed of little Interest and most foreign to students living in a rural island out in the middle of the Pacific. Ocean. During my tour, I visited many schools and talked to hundreds of students. I had some successful presentations but for the most part they were a difficult audience. It was while I was in Hawaii that my space science lecturer career came to an end. I was offered a position at the NASA Jet Propulsion Laboratory, (JPL)in Pasadena as the Manager of the Education Office. I accepted the position and my family and I headed back to California to assume a new job.

Jet Propulsion Laboratory (JPL)

JPL was and is a fascinating place to work. The laboratory is operated under contract to NASA by the California Institute of Technology, a highly-rated university known for its excellent staff and its teachings in Mathematics and Science. As a NASA center JPL was responsible for managing the exploration missions to the Moon and the Planets. It operates the Deep Space Network which is responsible tracking spacecraft that fly into deep space towards the planets.

JPL was very much involved in the exploration of the moon in anticipation of man landing on the moon, JPL designed and managed the Ranger unmanned flights to the moon. The Ranger spacecraft gave us the first close up pictures of the moon's surface prior to the Ranger crash landing. The Ranger missions were followed by the Surveyor missions. The surveyor was unique in that it was designed with a propulsion system that would slow down the craft and soft-land on the surface of the moon. It was a major accomplishment. The craft provided a multitude of photos and information on the nature of the surface of the moon. A total of seven surveyor spacecraft were launched all but two succeeded in landing at the designated target. Insert photo Conrad at Surveyor craft

As the Manager of the Education Office I was responsible for transferring new scientific knowledge acquired as a result of these missions to the educational community. To accomplish this task I managed a variety of initiatives. I produced a variety of educational products that summarized mission profiles and mission results. Colorful posters were created that illustrated the fabulous images of planets and moons observed by planetary missions. Printed materials such as pamphlets and bulletins were also produced for missions that were on going. Our office was also somewhat involved in producing documentary films related to specific missions.

On a daily basis, I and my staff conducted tours of laboratory facilities for students, teachers and professional organization as well as VIP visits. I was pleased to coordinate the visit for several interesting and famous people including Paul Newman, Ricardo Montalban, Ray Bradbury, some of the Apollo astronauts and in one instance, Prince Charles of England.

I also organized educational conferences for educators during the Viking planetary landings and at the time when planetary spacecraft Martian landing and close planetary encounters with the planets Jupiter and Saturn.

CHAPTER 13

THE GOLDEN DECADE OF PLANETARY EXPLORATION

VIKING I AND 2 SPACECRAFT

THE VIKING PROJECT THE EXPLORATION OF MARS

NASA's Viking Project found a place in history when it became the first U.S. mission to land a spacecraft safely on the surface of Mars and return images of the surface. Two identical spacecraft, each consisting of a lander and an orbiter, were built. Each orbiter-lander pair flew together and entered Mars orbit; the landers then separated and descended to the planet's surface.

The Viking 1 lander touched down on the western slope of Chryse Planitia (the Plains of Gold), while the Viking 2 lander settled down at Utopia Planitia.

Besides taking photographs and collecting other science data on the Martian surface, the two landers conducted three biology experiments designed to look for possible signs of life. These experiments discovered unexpected and enigmatic chemical activity in the Martian soil, but provided no clear evidence for the presence of living microorganisms in soil near the landing sites. According to scientists, Mars is self-sterilizing. They believe the combination of solar ultraviolet radiation that saturates the surface, the extreme dryness of the soil and the oxidizing nature of the soil chemistry prevent the formation of living organisms in the Martian soil. The Viking mission was planned to continue for 90 days after landing. Each orbiter and lander operated far beyond its design lifetime. Viking Orbiter 1 continued for four years and 1,489 orbits of Mars, concluding its mission August 7, 1980, while Viking Orbiter 2 functioned until July 25, 1978. Because of the variations in available sunlight, both landers were powered by radioisotope thermoelectric generators -- devices that create electricity from heat given off by the natural decay of plutonium. That power source allowed long-term science investigations that otherwise would not have been possible. Viking Lander 1 made its final transmission to Earth November 11, 1982. The last data from Viking Lander 2 arrived at Earth on April 11, 1980

I was assigned to travel to Mexico City to do Spanish TV voiceover for the Mars Landing in 1975. I had scheduled an educators conference to be conducted at the laboratory. It was one of the activities that I did for educators bringing them close to the action during planetary exploration. The landing on Mars had been delayed a few times, in those days we did not have the benefit of emails so much of my communication with teachers was by using telegrams. The decision to send me to Mexico was made after it was decided that the video of landing on Mars would be uplifted to satellite in distributed worldwide. There was a need for Spanish-speaking person to go to Mexico City and describe events they were unfolding. I was assigned to fulfill that mission by Bill Nixon from NASA headquarters and he was given the task of coordinating the educational conference at JPL that was to be attended by 300 educators from all fifty states.

I had little time to prepare for this television program to be conducted in Mexico City. I gathered a few photographs and I took with me a small scale models of the Viking spacecraft and I flew to Mexico City. I was greeted at the airport by dignitaries from Televisa, the major broadcasting network in the Spanish-speaking world . We immediately gathered and formulated plans for the Mars landing broadcast that would occur the next morning at 5 o'clock in the morning.

On the day of the Mars landing I arrived at the Televisa studio at 4:00 in the morning. I was immediately informed that I could not wear a light blue shirt I was wearing. The reason being was that my program host was also wearing a light blue shirt and he felt uncomfortable with me wearing the same color of shirt. I informed the director that I had traveled from California and I had a limited wardrobe, and no extra shirts. Without further discussion, we went on the air at 4:30 in the morning.

Televisa is a major television network in the Spanish speaking world. Its programs reach the U. S. Mexico, Central America and South America.

The Viking 1 arrived on Mars on schedule and landed gently on the surface of Mars shortly after 5 o'clock in the morning on July 20,1975. The Mars images from the spacecraft of the surface of Mars were received in Pasadena via the deep space network. Dr. Hibbs, was the TV host in the Blue Room at the Jet Propulsion Laboratory. His commentary and images were uplifted to a satellite and distributed worldwide including Mexico. I would take his English commentary and translated into Spanish and add additional discussion as I felt appropriate.

We were all very excited and with great anticipation waited to see the first hand the surface of Mars the camera on the spacecraft would construct the image slowly by scanning vertically forgot to bottom and slowly developed a Martian landscape in front of the spacecraft. Slowly the surface of Mars was revealed to humanity then called the red planet by earthbound observers, the surface of Mars was indeed red. We conducted a three-hour television broadcast listened to expert geologist describe and interpret the various views of the planet and trying to interpret the nature of the surface. It was indeed an exciting moment in the exploration of the planet and we were sharing it with the entire world. This was only the beginning!

Following the television program. I was invited by the American ambassador to the embassy to small gathering with local dignitaries and government officials. They were all most complimentary of the TV program and of course of the successful landing on Mars. The following day I returned to Pasadena and continued to be amazed by the Mars images we were receiving from the surface of Mars.

Another responsibility while at JPL was to be the legal custodian of the lunar rock sample collected during the Apollo 11 mission. This involved coordinating exhibit sites and insure that adequate security for the moon sample while it was displayed and secure storage when not on display.

One memorable bone rock exhibit took place in Oaxaca Mexico. The bone rock was to be exhibited in conjunction with the opening of a new planetarium in the city of Oaxaca. Oaxaca is a city located south of Mexico City. I personally flew the little sample from Los Angeles to Mexico City and later the city of Oaxaca. This is a bit complicated. It requires me to stay in Mexico City overnight says there was no service into Oaxaca on the same day. Arranging for security in Mexico City was a bit of a nightmare. Additionally, when the Mexico City airport director heard the moon rock was arriving he requested to have a special viewing for him and his staff. When we landed in Mexico City the pilot called my name and asked to come to the front of the plane.

Waiting for me would two soldiers that were to accompany me to the main floor of the airport. As we walked down the corridors of the airport people staring at me I must've look like some criminal type. They directed me to small table cordoned and off to keep the public at a distance. I opened the case containing a lunar rock. I extracted the pyramid shaped acrylic container made to hold the sample. The airport manager and his staff came in to observe the lunar sample. "Que bonita pierdita" what a pretty little rock he said. He thanked me and walked away. I packed the moon sample, two police cars were awaiting me, with sirens blasting I was driven off to my hotel. The sample was placed in the large safe in the basement of the hotel. One police officer led me to a secure room instructed an officer spend the night guarding my hotel door.

The next morning with equal fanfare the two guards and two police cars with sirens wailing I was transported back to the airport. I got a flight that would take me to the city of Oaxaca. My arrival at the airport was most interesting. Unbeknown to me a band was awaiting my arrival. As people deplaned the band started playing only to be hushed by the Governor of the state of Oaxaca. As I emerged from the plane the band started playing. It appears the band was intended for my arrival! After a very gracious greeting of welcome I was driven to the police department weapon storage. Here is where the lunar sample was securely stored. It would be displayed the following day for the opening of a new planetarium.

During the display of the moon rock exhibit, I made a presentation describing in detail the gathering of the moon rock by the Apollo 11 astronauts.

The Governor assigned a driver to be my guide and to show me some of the more interesting features of the Oaxaca region. Oaxaca is located in the southwestern part of Mexico. It is bordered by the states of Guerreros to the west and Puebla to the northwest, Veracruz to the north and Chiapas to the east, To the south of Oaxaca has a significant coastline on the Pacific Ocean.

The state is best known 14 indigenous people of cultures. The most humorous and best known by others up or text and I missed text but there are 16 cultures that are officially recognized these cultures have survived better than most others in Mexico due to the states rugged and isolated terrain. Most live in the Central Valley region which is also an important area for tourism attracting people for his archaeological sites such as Monte Alban, its native culture and crafts. Another important tourist area is the coast which is a major resort of Huatulco. Oaxaca is also one of the most biologically diverse states in Mexico ranking in the top three along with Chiapas, and Veracruz for numbers of rentals against mammals and plants.

While employed at JPL another significant mission was a voyager project. This project what was having difficulty getting funded by Congress. One of my projects related tasks was to generate public support from the educational community. Through the education conference at the lab we had developed support of educators and planetarium director for the various projects conducted by JPL. I contacted the educational community and asked them to contact their Senators and congressmen in support of the Voyager Project. I could not measure the level of influence they had on their representatives, suffice it to say the Voyager project was approv3d for funding by congress.

The spacecraft were built by JPL and launched on gravity assist trajectory to encounter the planets Jupiter, Saturn, Uranus and Neptune.

The primary mission was the exploration of Jupiter and Saturn. After making a string of discoveries there — such as active volcanoes on Jupiter's moon Io and intricacies of Saturn's rings — the mission was extended. Voyager 2 went on to explore Uranus and Neptune, and is still the only spacecraft to have visited those outer planets. The adventurers' current mission, the Voyager Interstellar Mission (VIM), will explore the outermost edge of the Sun's domain. And beyond.

The twin Voyager 1 and 2 spacecraft are exploring where nothing from Earth has flown before. Continuing their more-than-40-year journey since their 1977 launches, they each are much farther away from Earth and the sun than Pluto. In August 2012, Voyager 1 made the historic entry into interstellar space, the region between stars, filled with material ejected by the death of nearby stars millions of years ago. Voyager 2 entered interstellar space on November 5, 2018 and scientists hope to learn more about this region. Both spacecraft are still sending scientific information about their surroundings through the Deep Space Network, or DSN.

That being the case Carl Sagan was instrumental in creating an artifact on the spacecraft that contained information about the earth and its inhabitants. It was decided that a videodisc which had tremendous storage capacity would be mounted on the spacecraft. A selection of photographs that represented various aspects of the earth and its people were encoded on the disc. Additionally, greetings in various languages were recorded on the disc.

As Carl Sagan has noted, *"The spacecraft will be encountered and the record played only if there are advanced spacefaring civilizations in interstellar space. But the launching of this bottle into the cosmic ocean says something very hopeful about life on this planet."*

The following are a few examples of greetings recorded on the disc:

Akkadian
"May all be very well"
Amoy (Min dialect)
"Friends of space, how are you all, have you eaten yet? Come visit us if you have time"
Arabic
"Greetings to our friends in the stars, we wish that we will meet someday"
Aramaic
"Peace"
English
"Hello from the children of the planet earth"
Spanish
"Hello and greetings to all"
Cantonese
"Hi. How are you? Wish you peace, health and happiness"

I envisioned using videodisc technology as a more efficient vehicle for mass dissemination of visual information to the educational community. I approached NASA Headquarters with a plan to archive mission results and photos on videodisc and distribute it to educators nationwide. NASA was not enthused so I started exploring ways of using videodisc technology in education.

During this time, I *was* approached by a small group of young entrepreneurs from New Jersey that were exploring ways of using this technology in education. Their ideas were consistent with what I had previously proposed to NASA.

I had been involved in the excitement of the Viking landing on Mars. The Voyager missions were equally exciting. I had organized an educational conference at Cape Kennedy at the time of the rocket launch of Voyager 1. My office conducted conferences at the time when the spacecraft's closest approach to Jupiter and later during Saturn's closest approach. These events were very well attended we felt we had truly involved educators in the excitement of planetary exploration. I met many dedicated science teachers, university professors and planetarium directors, all grateful to be in close proximity of the events of planetary exploration as they unfolded at the Jet Propulsion Laboratory.

I organized two symposia titled **"Jupiter and the Mind of Men" and "Saturn and the mind of Men".** These symposia were conducted just prior of close encounter at Jupiter and Saturn. Program speakers included, Carl Sagan, from Cornel University, Phil Morrison, from MIT. Ray Bradbury, author, and Arthur C. Clark, author, and other scientists involved in the various experiment aboard the spacecraft.

I thought it would make for an interesting and stimulating evening if I mixed science fiction authors with a group of planetary scientists. Thus, I extended an invitation to Ray Bradbury, who lived in Los Angeles and Arthur C,

Clark, who at the time was living in Sri Lanka, both graciously accepted my invitation. Arthur C. Cark informed me that because the United States barred the SST from flying over the US, he would never set foot in the US of A. He became even more interesting with this comment.

I started exploring how I could bring Sir Clark, via video into the Beckman Auditorium at Cal Tec. In those days satellite was in its infancy, it was not at the turnkey level. It required considerable technical coordination. Through the efforts of my talented colleague, Mr. Phil Neuhauser, he arranged for a UPI crew in SriLanka to setup a satellite uplink in Mr Clark backyard and we set up a downlink at the symposium site. At the appropriate time in the program, I introduced Sir Clark and he appeared on a large screen from his backyard in Sri Lanka! It was magnificent to hear him live, sharing his thoughts on the momentous upcoming events. The audience was most impress with the presentations during the program and hearing Sir Clark in a live presentation was a real bonus.

A pleasant surprise that night was the unexpected visit of young Governor Brown. He was a supporter of NASA programs. I introduced to the audience and he made some brief remarks on the impact of new knowledge on humanity. It was a memorable night for the 1200 space enthusiasts in the audience. Manager at JPL. I considered myself fortunate to have been involved in some of America's greatest missions of the exploration of our solar system. The next Voyager encounter at the planet Uranus was to occur in1989. It seemed like a long time to wait.

CHAPTER 14

MY LASERVIDEO DISC ADVENTURE

I was ready for a new adventure. Desk top computers were rapidly evolving and various technologies were beginning to make an impact in the educational arena. I became aware and enthused about the capabilities of the videodisc on board of the Voyager spacecraft. I was interested in bringing this technology to education.

Videodisc offered features which at the time seemed an ideal medium for the classroom. A videodisc has tremendous storage capacity. Each side of a disc can store 52,000 images, so a single two sided disc can store 104,000 images. A disc can provide 30 minutes of full motion video. A very appealing features of this technology is random access to stored information. Each image has a unique, and by using a handheld remote control unit, one could enter the unique number of an image in one second or two the images will appear on the screen.

It is also possible to access a single frame (picture) within a motion picture sequence. Motion sequences can be played at various slow motion speeds either forward or backwards. These features make it a powerful teaching tool.

A laserdisc player could be connected to a computer with a simple interphase thus creating a technology able to create interactive learning lessons as well as interactive public displays. The vast storage of visuals gave a teacher many opportunities to create individual instructional programs for students.

I joined a small company who had previously approached with their vision of its educational applications. The three entrepreneurs were, Bill Clark, Betty Paxton, and Ralph Heigle. They had started a company called Video

Vision, later the name changed to Optical Data Corporation. I assumed the position of Senior Vice President and became the evangelist, for this technology in the educational community. Leon Andors an executive in the print industry was an early investor. While we were low on capital, we were all endowed with loads of enthusiasm, creativity, drive and a great desire to succeed.

Our initial goal was to was to take the photographs and motion sequence is generated by various NASA missions store them in laser disk and market them to the educational community. This is a monumental task to begin with we had to acquire the photos from NASA. Since these were under the public domain we did not have to pay for the photos. Once the laborious task of acquiring the photos, each frame had to be shut individually along with archiving the visuals on the disk we had create directories which included the frame or photo number and a brief description of each photo

Our company produced numerous laser disks related to Space missions. . Our first product was the Voyager Project disk. Later we produced on the Apollo mission to the moon. The significance of these productions was that we were making the vast amounts of visual information resulting from these missions into the hands of teachers and students. Most of this visual material was stored in warehouses in Washington DC and not readily available to education or the public

Marketing this technology into the educational marketplace was a significant challenge. Being a small company we did not have a large marketing budget. Frequently, we are facing very severe money problems. My partners asked if I had any contacts that could provide us with some financial resources. While at JPL I had the occasion to work with Cal Tech development office. An individual that I knew from this office had moved to the Arco Foundation in Los Angeles, this foundation was created by the Ridgefield Oil Company.

I set up a meeting with him at the foundation office in Los Angeles. At the time, we were in production of an earth science disc. Company Atlantic Richfield Corporation a giant oil producing company I thought they may be interested in providing financial resources to the education product relevant to geology. He was most receptive. I requested $25,000. He asked me to write a two-page proposal and the one page budget. We anxiously prepared the proposal and I hand carried it to his office. A few days later I heard from him informing me that the foundation was so impressed with work that they had double a request to $50,000. The check was delivered to our New Jersey office a few days later. We were happy campers. We had been given the financial save at a most timely moment. As a small company, we encountered several financial cliffs that made our success difficult and tested our wills. However, we manage to survive and succeed in moving forward in the development of educational products in this very new technology.

Implementing a new technology in the field of education was not an easy task. As a general rule, new technologies in 1985 were somewhat threatening to educators. Textbooks had always been the standard tool for teachers, and video disc were perceived as a technology that would replace the old textbook. Teachers were hesitant about abandoning the comfortable textbook.

To accelerate the implementation of our products we attended and displayed our product at many education conferences. We made conferences presentations illustrating the classroom use of these marvelous products. We established pilot sites in school districts so we could have practitioners that could speak with authority to fellow teachers about the effectiveness of this technology in both teaching and student learning. we were convinced that video discs were the appropriate technology for the video generation for the students in the classrooms of America

Book publishing companies were not enthused about laser video discs. They saw them as a threat to the world of textbook adoption. School districts and entire states adopted textbooks. This was always a big financial bonanza for publishers. We have a reasonable success in marketing our products to school districts that considers themselves as innovative and early adopters of new technology the sales were usually slow and time-consuming. We felt we needed to increase your sales by entering the realm of adoption of school products.

Our company was fortunate in that we had employed, Mr. Ron Reed a gentleman who was very familiar with the adoption process in the state of Texas. We had produced an exciting elementary science program called "Windows on Science". Web decided to submit this elementary science product for adoption in the state of Texas. I might add that our disks had narration both English and Spanish narration, with the growth of Spanish-speaking students in the United States we felt this was a definite advantage over text books written in English only. Additionally, our video discs had thousands of content related pictures, motion video sequences and a most comprehensive teacher manuals. These features made them powerful teaching tool for a generation of students that were accustomed to video and visual learning. Videodisc technology offers features that makes it a powerful teaching tool in the hands of a teacher.

Connected to computer with the simple interface, this technology can be programed for interactive individualized learning programs.

The first obstacle we encountered was that the state of Texas adoption laws were created to adopt textbooks and made no provisions for funding or the adoption of any kind of technology. Fortunately, for us Texas school officials were enthused by laser disk technology and the law was modified to allow school district to purchase laser disks, laser disk players as well as textbooks. Optical data Corporation made history. We had created an educational technology product that met the educational prerequisites that allowed it to be adapted like a textbook. Texas was the first state to implement an educational technology state wide. We were most happy with our success in having a statewide adoption of of our programs in this technology.

I continued working as Senior Vice President, at Optical Data Corp from 1982 to 1989 and I preached the Laserdisc technology gospel, all over the country. Our little company had grown from the four founding members, to a full video production and marketing company to over one hundred employees. We continued our production efforts and produced laser discs in Astronomy, Physical Science, Biology, chemistry, and Mathematics. Optical Data was well on its way to being a prime producer of educational technology products.

After several rounds of venture capital funding the company was acquired by Cox cable and later by the publisher of McGraw-Hill. The publisher had no interest in further development of laser video disc technology. I suspect they acquired it to eliminate the textbook competition, sadly Optical Data Corporation faded into the past. The immergence of the internet further accelerated the demise of laserdisc technology. I left the company in 1990. I was recruited by Hughes Electronics to head up a project to develop interactive elementary educational television programs to be delivered by it was 1989 the new television technology of DIRECTV.

CHAPTER 15

The Galaxy Classroom
DIRECTV at Hughes Electronicsughes
Electronics Hugh HH

It was 1989 we will well on our way to having a statewide videodisc adoption in the state of Texas. I got an interesting call from a headhunter in Los Angeles. The person informed me that a company was looking for an individual knowledgeable in the implementation of technology in America's classrooms, it sounded interesting so I decided I would listen to what they had to offer both in terms of job opportunity and the educational technology project

I met with the placement agency representative in a hotel near Los Angeles airport. She was pleasant and described a project as a television project yet to be defined. She queried me on implementing technology in schools. I described the pilot sites I had established as part of our implementation strategy for our laser disk project.

After further discussion, she finally revealed that it was Hughes Electronics the company interested in establishing a DirecTV channel for delivering of educational programming into schools. That peak my interest.

I was familiar with Hughes electronics from my days at JPL. We used to say, "Hughes is very good but expensive!". Hughes had been involved in designing and building spacecraft for JPL. They pioneered communication satellites and built the first synchronous communication satellite, placed in a synchronous orbit 22,000 miles above the equator. Hughes built the Surveyor spacecraft that self-landed on the moon and the Pioneers spacecraft which were very successful projects for NASA in the 1960s

She then arranged for me to be interviewed by the man in charge of the project Mr. Norm Avrech. Mister Avrech was an experienced engineer at Hughes. He had been assigned to explore the ways DirecTV could be used in the educational arena. DirecTV was fairly new and in its early days of implementation.

I was quite interested in the fact that an aerospace company was interested in entering the realm of education. I was aware of Hughes being an aerospace giant and known for its reputation of excellence. This immediately elevated my expectations. I had a pleasant interview. He described his activities in the somewhat unidentified educational project. He had proceeded cautiously and had met with many educators nationwide and got excellent advice from many professionals. He was not an educator, and was very thorough in his research. I admire his diligence and method of operation. I felt I could work with him in this ambitious but somewhat undefined project. After a lengthy discussion he offered me and I accepted the position of executive director of the pilot project. I drove south to Huntington beach on a crowded 405 San Diego Freeway very much elated about my new challenge on anew project at Hughes Electronics.

I gave notice of my resignation of my position at Optical Data Corporation. My partners were not pleased about my resignation. I felt the company was well on its way to being successful and my presence was no longer critical to its success. Another factor was that Hughes offered me a salary that was double what I was earning at Optical Data. I completed my final assignment by attending educational technology conference in Hawaii. While my wife and I were in route, the Hotel Union, in Hawaii went on strike. The conference was canceled. I informed the Optical Data of the cancellation. The company was generous and gave us a bonus vacation. Janet and I spent a wonderful week in Oahu in anticipation of my new position with Hughes Electronics.

On April 1, 1989, I reported for work at Hughes electronics in El Segundo California 35 miles from my home in Huntington Beach. I met with Mr. Avrech to discuss my role in the project. An advisory committee had been formed made up of former superintendents career educators which provided interesting insight about educational technology and its implementation. At this time the project was quite undefined. His primary motivation was to create more student interest in careers in engineering and science. Hughes being a company that marketed it satellite building service to many countries, saw a need for employees that could speak a foreign language. It was a forward looking investment in the future of the company.

What grade level and what curriculum areas would be developed was my first question.

Those issues had not been decided. He asked if I had any thoughts on that aspects of the project. Based on my extensive contact with elementary schools, I suggested that the greatest need was in upper elementary level. During the time I was with NASA as a lecturer I visited many elementary schools that had somewhat limited science programs. Additionally, I had observed the teachers at the elementary level had a somewhat limited science training. Teaching science was not their favorite subject. I suspected that their limited background inhibited them from creative science teaching. At the same time, I was convinced that students at the upper elementary level were full of curiosity and willing to pursue science learning if presented in an interesting and engaging manner.

I was most emphatic on creating a high quality television programs with the engaging content. I was opposed to talking heads TV programs. I suggested the budget of $20,000 a minute production cost. Hughes was going to fund the program. My suggested budget of $12 million was beyond their financial expectation.

My strategy for funding and additional $12 million I hired a professional proposal writer. We prepared a proposal and submitted it to the National Science Foundation. After exerting a bit of political pressure, the National Science Foundation gave us a grand for $5 million. We needed an additional $7 or $8 million. WE were successful in getting additional funding from the Winegard Foundation. We were on our way!

Hughes was also very interested in attracting minority students into science engineering in keeping with that objective, I suggested language arts was important since it would strengthen student writing reading and comprehension. Minority students came to schools speaking a foreign language and so reading and writing was always an obstacle to learning.

From a marketing point of view, I felt that elementary schools were indeed a larger market. Furthermore, my experience in implementing technology I found elementary schools to be more receptive about implementing new technology in the classroom. From this discussion in was later decided we would produce television programs in science and language arts for upper elementary schools.

The project hired Tippy Fortune, a television producer that has been involved in the production of a successful Sesame Street children's television program. She was designated as a person to lead the video production efforts for the project. The science specialist was from Seattle Washington he has vast experience in science education and Dr. Mitsy Lewis and was also an experienced educator in the field of language arts. Both were most helpful in working with the video production companies in designing the hands-on science and language arts television program.

Earlier as we were brainstorming with educator groups we concluded we would design and network quality television program that generated interaction from students and promoted hands-on learning activities in the classroom the television series would have an engaging story line that would peak student interests. Embedded in the programs will problems presented to students. After viewing the weekly television program the students as part of the classroom activity would create solutions to problems presented in the TV program. .We designed hands-on activities and classroom discussion the student solutions would be prepared on paper and fax back to our staff. Some of the student solutions would then be integrated in the following week television program. I called this asynchronous interaction. This was a different from the typical interactive educational programs that demanded instant reaction from the students. My thinking was that asynchronous interaction allowed for students and teachers to work on solutions as classroom activities. They have a whole week to working solutions and then submit their solutions to us via fax transmissions. Some schools with Internet capability would send the solutions to us via email.

This strategy worked extremely well for students and teachers. The video programs for high-quality production, and the curriculum demanded a lot of classroom hands-on activities. These features were most motivating for students. Their motivation was further enhanced when they saw their solutions and their names on the television programs .It gave the students in the school great pride to see their own names, their work, the name of their school on the television broadcast.

I have had experience in implementing new technology in my previous work with laser video discs in schools. I decided that we would set up pilot schools strategically located throughout the United States. We also set up schools in Juarez, Mexico. The program narrations were broadcasted in English and Spanish. Our goal was to set up pilot sites in urban inner-city sites as well as rural areas.

We provided the schools in the selected target areas with a description of our program and asked them to submit a proposal on how they would implement the program in their schools. Our goal was to set up 40 pilot sites

We agreed to provide the pilot schools with computers television sets video recorders fax machines and wire the classrooms for Internet and video distribution we provided a direct TV satellite dish

The selected pilot schools were required to provide teachers dedicated to utilizing our program in their science and language arts program. The school districts were required to pay travel expenses to our training session for teachers and one parent representative this was a substantial commitment for schools with limited budgets

We were most pleased to receive close to 200 proposals. We selected 40 pilot sites. I was pleased that we selected an excellent proposal submitted by the elementary school near my hometown in Los Ojos, New Mexico.

My next step was for me to arrange for various contractors to wire the school and purchase, ship and install the equipment in the schools.

The wiring of the schools was an interesting and challenging task. It involved about 30 contractors some of which had never worked with schools. Working out installation schedules to coincide with daily school schedules proved to be the most laborious task. By December 1994 we have completed all the wiring of 40 schools. We have trained about 100 teachers and the video production of the upper grade science series was done. Our plan was to start broadcasting and implementing the program in 40 school sites in January 1995.

The video production was coordinated by Tippy Fortune. We hired WGBH a well-respected PBS station in Boston to produce the science series. We also employed WQED in Pittsburgh a PBS station to produce the language arts program for the lower elementary grades.

I called the project The Galaxy Classroom. Hughes satellites were designated as Galaxy satellites. The Galaxy Classroom Project was a huge success. From the original 40 pilot sites, we grow to 700 schools the second year of operation.

After doing extensive t marketing research I decided that the state of Georgia would be an ideal state to implement the Galaxy Classroom Project on a state-wide basis. The governor of Georgia had install the traditional large satellite dishes in all their schools. I managed to get a meeting with the Governor's staff. I mention that as part of our implementation we would install direct satellite dishes in all their schools. This intended installation concerned the governor. They had spent state funds to install traditional light satellite dishes and all other schools. So, I suggested that we could utilize their satellite dishes and the Georgia public television for delivering our programs. We would install one direct TV dish at Georgia public television site in Atlanta, We would download our program to the Georgia public television system, they would then rebroadcast using this system and their installed satellite dishes. This really please the governor. The Georgia education Department bought the program for 400 of their elementary schools.

No one had ever succeeded or attempted to provide student interactive instructional TV programs. We were providing interactive science and language arts instruction over 100,000 students our program was the first to offer a very high quality interactive television program delivered by DirecTV. We felt the program has great potential. Teachers loved our approach and students were truly engaged in science and language arts instruction. Personally, I was excited about the success of the implementation of the program. Our staff was excited our program design was warmly accepted by the educational community. We hired Rockmon Et Al, an independent evaluation company from San Francisco to conduct a program evaluation.

After two years of operation were delivering instruction to about 800 schools nationwide and two schools in Juarez, Mexico. We had hopes for expanding the program in the future, into more schools and more curriculum areas. I felt we were on our way!

But it was not to be. . A new CEO arrived at Hughes electronics, he did not believe Hughes electronic should be involved in education. He felt it was not part of our core business and he instructed us to sell the program. We had created and had been operating under a nonprofit entity the Galaxy Institute so technically we are not part of Hughes Electronics but, we were partially funded by the company. I tried to convince our staff for us to continue the operation as a nonprofit entity. Nobody was enthused about that idea. The program was sold to one of the major publishers and it died within the year. This was the second time a program I was involved in creating an innovative educational technology program, that was acquired and then killed by major publishing company. After six-year employment, we all went our separate ways. We were saddened to see our hard work disappear in the bureaucracy of a text book publisher, I guess they feared the competition of video curriculum that would not require textbooks was not in their best interest

I went to work for Hager Sharp Inc. a marketing firm in Washington DC. This company we hired to help us launch and market Galaxy Classroom. They specialized in creating marketing programs for educational technology companies. Hager sharp liked my experience in education and educational technology industry. They offered that me a position as vice president for the firm. I was involved in creating marketing campaigns for companies such as Zenith Corporation and Phillips Electronics. I was there for three years and then went onto semi- retirement status. At this time, my forty year career in educational technology and science education came to an end.

As a young boy, I had observed a magnificent spot on a ridge with a beautiful view of the Brazos Cliffs. I dreamed of someday building a home on this spot, with this magnificent view

Janet at our vacation home in Los Ojos, New Mexico

BUILDING OUR DREAM

A few years later, my Uncle Pantaleon, my father's brother bought this property. He was contemplating retirement so offered to buy this property which included about 30 acres of land. For a few years, we would visit the site and dream about a home. On one of these occasions, my sister Belinda, informed me that she had lined up a contractor to start building our house. We had a friend architect and she had designed the home in anticipation of us building it. The construction started in June of 1992. I always wanted a basement, so that was the first step. Construction moved along slowly. Because of the cold and snowy winters, construction stopped during the winter months. We spent our first Christmas in the house in 1995.The house was not completely finished but we thoroughly enjoyed our first Christmas in our dream house. Since that day we have spent many days in Los Ojos, enjoying the pleasant summers and spending time with my brothers and sisters.

My brothers and sisters
From left to right: Tom, Joanne, Teofila, Benito, Belinda, Teodoro(Ted) Rosenaldo, (Ross, Pablo
From left to right youngest to oldest

My family : sitting my daughter Chrisrine. Granddaughter, Julia, son inlaw, Michael, grandson Evan, Standing ,my daughter Michelle, grandson Matthew

Standing: Ben, Janet, Matthew Sitting: Julia, Evan holding Sofie

When I started working with NASA in 1964 I moved my family to Huntington Beach California. We bought a house next door to a lady who wrote is syndicated children's newspaper column known as ask Candy. Her name was Ellen Walpole Brooks. She started this column in 1994 when she lived in Boston. Through the years, the column was syndicated and had grown in popularity and increased in circulation. It appeared in about 90 newspapers throughout the United States and Canada.

At the time, I was employed by NASA as a space science lecturer. She came knocking at my door and asked if I worked for NASA. Her column was based on questions kids would submit to the local newspapers for the syndicated coma. This was 1964 , the space program was in the early stages and young people had a lot of questions about space exploration. She needed help, she wondered, if I was interested in helping her in writing and editing the column. Her audience was students from ages 9 to 15. At this age of children seem to be most curious about the world around them,

Ellen Walpole was a fascinating British lady. She has started private schools and had written several children's books including the first book about God and getting along the book for teenagers and others. I agreed to help her on A part-time basis. In time, as she grew older I ended up writing most of the columns myself.

The column was in existence for 32 years a tremendous amount of information that was generated responding to questions asked by the readership and provided by Ask Andy. The column appeared six days a week. Each daily column contained the answers for two questions that had been selected by Ms. Walpole and myself Each week we received about 10,000 questions from students all over the nation. The questions were as varied as young students inquiring imagination for example one question was: What is on the other side of darkness? How heavy is the moon? Does the stork really delivering babies? We could not possibly read or answer all the questions received each week. We divided the country into regions. Each week we would read all the mail from a single region from that mail we would select the most engaging questions. As an incentive to engage inquiry among students we worked with a publisher encyclopedias. Each day we would grant a set of encyclopedias to student whose question we selected I have received several letters from students now adults applauding the significant impact in their lives by the selection of the question and how much the set of encyclopedias had added to their educational endeavors.

I stopped writing the column in 1993. It had been syndicated since 1955 During the life of the column over 20,000 questions and answers had been published through the ninety newspapers that carried the syndicated column.

The world-wide web, the Internet came into public awareness in the early nineties. The internet is a magnificent depository for information. The Ask Andy content seemed ideal for the Internet. Ask Andy was published for a period of 34 years. The content of the column existed on 90,000 pages of text, stored in my garage. With the passing of Ellen Walpole, at the age of 92, I inherited the entire collection of articles and their copyright.

The Internet seemed the ideal home for the thousands of questions and answers we had written in response to student and adult questions. Of Scanning the material and convert it from paper version to a digital format. Beyond converting it to electronic format the content had to be edited and the copy cleaned up. I acquired a super scanner and started the scanning task in 2001. I split the task of scanning and editing and entering the column one of the time into a website called www.youandy.com that I had created to host the Ask Andy content. Is a tedious process. It took me ten years to scan and edit the entire 18,000 articles into the website www.youaskandy.com. The site became available to the public in 2010.

The website is extremely popular on the Internet. Each day it is visited by hundreds of warlike visitors mostly students resulting in over 1 million hits a month.

I continue to add information to the website. To give you an idea of the type of questions available I have included a few sample articles. These samples provide some insight of the type of questions in the minds of students of ages 9 to 15-year-olds. Additionally, I consider my creation of this website as an Internet educational resources available as a learning tool for students and adults on the entire planet. Each month the website is visited by over 500,000 learners.

Sample Articles available on the website:

How is thread made?

Submitted by a 13-year-old girl from Dodge City, Kansas?

Fred is made from strands of fibers. The fibers maybe cotton, silk, wool, linen, rayon nylon or other textile materials
Human first learn how to make shred as a result of success in spitting fibers for weaving.
We found that by twisting the fibers tightly we could make thread. The production of sewing thread involve the same basic steps as a production of yarn for weaving the sample fibers such as cotton or wool are cleaned and then combed until all fibers are smoothed out.

The thin, threadlike fibers are then rolled over and over to form thick coils. These coils are put in the drawing frame, where they pass between sets of powerful rollers. The rollers draw the fibers out and press them into thin ribbons.

The ribbons then go to another machine, called the doubling frame, that presses them into fine strips. The strips are folded over, and again drawn out

Next the strips are combed again to make the even in width. They bare then wound on bobbins. Several strands are twisted together to form a coarse yarn, which is twisted tightly into the finished thread.

Manufacturers then bleach or dye the thread, wind it on wooden pools or bobbins and send it out to stores.

Cotton ranks as the most widely used fiber for making thread. The long fiber Sea Island cotton makes the best thread.

Silks and manmade fibers such as nylon and rayon start out as filaments or extremely thin yarn. They do not need to be combed or pressed. The filament yarn is twisted directly into thread. Then it is bleached or dyed and wound onto spools.

Special characteristics of man-made fibers make them increasingly important in the field of thread. Perhaps the most outstanding quality of thread made from man-made fibers is that it has great strength and durability.

Thread made from man-made fibers offers higher resistance to seam failure than ordinary thread. Also, it makes possible higher sewing speeds. For these and a number of other good reasons, this type of thread is being used more and more today in the manufacture of shoes and clothing.

For most sewing uses, tread is drawn out to make a single strand. But for heavier sewing, manufactures twist two or more threads together to make two ply thread or heavier.

Humans first learned the art of weaving and perfected a system . of spinning fibers for use in weaving. It was later found that by twisting the fibers tightly, thread could be made. We learned to use the thread to sew garments together. Before we learned to sew with thread, we could only drape or tie fabric around our bodies.

Should you pick up a rabbit by sears?

Your bunny may be polite about this, but he certainly does not like being picked up by the ears. Nor is it good for him. Those long furry ears are made of grizzle and they're full of blood vessels and sensitive nerves. Though the ears are strong they can be damaged if you use them as handles, especially if the bunny is heavy the proper way to lift any pet, is to get your arm under the heaviest part of his body. This is usually his hindquarters. You may find it convenient to place a small pad or cushion on your arm. With a little patience and a carrot or two you can soon train your bunny to hop onto it hold him this way he is comfortable and close enough to study your face and listen well you talk to him.

Each month the website continues to attract thousands of visitors worldwide. The on-site survey poll indicates ask Andy is primarily visited by students and parents. It pleases me that you ask Andy he continues to be a resource for students with inquiring minds. I continue to add contents to be a learning resource for both adults and students. For a long time in the future. I will continue to add content and hopefully continue to motivate learners to seek knowledge by asking questions and seeking answers to their questions.

CHAPTER 16

A self-Made Man

No doubt you have heard people use the expression to describe the person who was triumphed economically, socially or politically, personally I do not indoors this concept no human is an island. Most individuals have had contact with experienced influenced from a wife, relatives, community people, teachers working colleagues, and of course parents. This individual all contribute to the making of a person. I'm willing to give credit to many people for my fulfillment in life as a "self-made man."

Here are a few individuals that I would like to credit for having a positive influence on my making it as a man.

I would like to start out with my father and mother. My parents were not educated people but they were very smart about life. The greatest contribution was the example They said for me they raised a family of nine kids Eddie's one of them became a productive citizen. We all graduated from high school and some of us will college-educated. I hasten to add that no one served as much as one minute in jail.

My father never went to school. I Admired his tenacity. Well we live in a small wrench anyway he was in constant hustle turn the financial resources to meet the needs of a large family. He raised hogs, cattle and at one time operated to dairy. During the second world or what most of the men in the community has been drafted there is a need for someone to provide firewood for families that relate on wood burning stoves for cooking and eating. My father 's other need and started selling firewood to families in the community. This turned out to be the most profitable endeavor. My father had an able crew, with me and my three brothers. We could produce several loads of wood each Saturday. Each load of wood was sold for eight dollars. This provided some cash flow during the slow winter months.

My father's constant effort to seek out ways of making a living was an inspiration to me as I made my way through life. When I arrived at New Mexico State University to start my college career I had $77 and my pocket. Not enough money to even pay for one semester of tuition. In my heart, I knew I could somehow find work to pay for my educational expenses. I worked at mowing lawns, housecleaning for two older ladies, as a waiter at a restaurant, a dishwasher and finally a cook at the University canteen. All these other jobs contributed to a meager existence. My father did not have the resources to support me and my educational costs. Through diligent efforts I was able to pay for my living and educational expenses. Through diligent effort, I was able to pay for my living and college expenses. The key words here are diligence, self-discipline and a desire to succeed, all inspired by my parents.

The models during my educational use from elementary to high school all my teachers were similar in one respect. They all had great expectations of me. Each went gave me confidence that I could succeed in my educational endeavors. It did not matter that I came from as it was called in those days economically deprived background yes, we were poor but that never gave our teachers the notion that we could not learn and not succeed. My high school teachers made it infinitely clearer to me that I must get a college education. This was a realistic expectation that in my mind was totally achievable the end result, I went to college and completed a bachelors and a Master's degree.

Growing up our neighbors were a childless couple named Mr. and Mrs. Fred Sierra. He was originally from Colorado and he appeared to be a better educated than the average local rancher. My parents selected him to be my sponsor my Padrino or Godfather for my confirmation. Up until I started school are used to spend a lot of time at their home. She used to bake cakes and lots of cookies which are always a great incentive for young boy. As I grew older I begin to admire Mr. Fred Sierra public speaking abilities. He had a great deep resonant speaking voice and a wonderful command of both English and Spanish languages. I first became aware of his voice and delivery when he read the passion of Christ during the Holy Thursday mass and during other Lenten rituals. His deep voice rang through the church and made the reading of the passion come to life.

In those days, political rallies were conducted at the local Dancehall. The rallies were conducted following the Roberts rules of order. Mr. Sierra was always selected as chairman. He always conducted the political rally meetings with great dignity and decorum. He was a vibrant leader in other community events as he guided the adults to the fund-raising activities for the nascent St. Joseph Parochial school. He was my confirmation sponsor, he was indeed an admired Godfather or Padrino!

I greatly admired in his public speaking skills. When I was earning a living as a public speaker delivering presentations on space exploration to audiences all over this country and because of my fluency in Spanish I made presentations in Mexico Central and South America. Mr. Sierra made me a better speaker by the example set.

REFLECTIONS

I have had a most interesting life. As I approach my mid 80s my perspective on life has evolved and my appreciation for people with whom I have been associated has been greatly enhanced.

I have a great regard for my family. And by my family I mean extended family that includes uncles cousins and families of my cousins. In my youth, my extended family included uncles and aunts on my mother side and my father's side. My mother came from a large family and so that accounted for several uncles aunts cousins and most of them lived nearby.

Those relative extended a great deal of love and affection to us kids. Today none of my uncles and uncles are alive and I miss them. I now realize how much they enriched my childhood days. The family dinners, the weddings, the arrival of new cousins, some of them sad others joyful, made a most memorable childhood. When we causally strolled into my aunts and uncles homes, at all-times of day, if it was lunchtime or dinner time it didn't matter sat down and ate no invitations needed.

I grew up in a family of nine siblings. Four of them are gone. My older brother Paul, Ross, Ted, my older sister Belinda and Josephine, are gone. As a young kid, I used to hang out with my older brother Ted. He was four years older than I but, he tolerated me hanging around with him. His wife Julia is a wonderful one person and his two daughters Elaine and Angie are equally lovely. My sister Belinda is older than I died of cancer in 1999. She was my best friend. She and her husband will responsible for managing the construction our magnificent vacation home. My sister Josephine mentioned earlier it died as a child in 1948. In today's world jobs places us many miles away from our childhood home. I still look forward to returning to New Mexico and see younger brother,Tom and my wo sisters Joanne and Teofila. I visit them as often as I can. My two daughters barely know my nephews and nieces and cousins we seldom see each other so we have not shared family events in the ways that I did as a child

I'm also grateful for all the teachers I've had in life. My high school teachers, were all dedicated and most caring. The nuns were great disciplinarians with a form of discipline that was predictable and applied uniformly with great consistency. My high school teachers served as great models. The men always dressed in a shirt and tie and presented themselves in the most professional manner. I see teachers today dressed in Bermuda shorts and T-shirts. I don't believe that projects an image of professionalism that a student is expected to respect and behave in their presents with quiet and respectful demeanor.

Most importantly, my teachers had great expectations of all of us. Our economics status was never an issue. Yes, we were poor and we were Hispanics and they always conveyed the expectation that we could learn and succeed in life as adults regardless of our childhood status.

I distinctly remember my history teacher Mr. J.R. Martinez who wrote in my yearbook, "be sure you get a college education that was the most meaningful command laced with expectation

My high school graduation class was small, if I remember correctly we were 20 graduates. I was the valedictorian and at least five of my fellow graduates completed college degrees. I credit my teachers with giving us the motivation and confidence that we could continue to advance our education and succeed in whatever we chose as a life endeavor.

I have heard most people hate their jobs, I was fortunate to have the following jobs that I thoroughly enjoyed in my 37 years of employment.

Northern New Mexico College, Science Instructor (4 years)
NASA Headquarters/Oklahoma State University, Space Science Lecturer, Associate Professor (8 years)
NASA/ Jet Propulsion Laboratory, Manager, Educational Programs (10 Years)
Optical Data Corporation, Vice President, (8 years)
Hughes Electronics, Executive Director Galaxy Classroom Project (7 years)
Hager Sharpe Inc. Vice President (5 years)

I can honestly say, I enjoyed and succeeded in all my jobs. My appreciation for my jobs were two reasons, the people with whom I worked, and the type of work I was doing. All my occupations have been related to science. I started out as a science instructor, my career path stayed on educational technology and promoting science education

My work was always involved in opening new areas of learning and teaching strategies in education. As a teacher, I always strived to open windows of new knowledge for my students. When I was with NASA and JPL I was bringing the excitement of new knowledge resulting from space exploration to both students and teachers. These were very exciting times; the audiences were most receptive to the subject of space exploration.

Doing my years with Optical Data Corporation I was introducing to educators the capacity of a new technology of laser video discs. A powerful teaching tool and information resource, connecting laser disk to laptop computers, offered a new dimension in both teaching and learning.

At Hughes Electronics, I had the challenge of bringing for the first time to the classrooms of America a asynchronous interactive, high quality television programs, delivered by the new technology of DirecTV. It illustrated the power of technology by delivering instruction to over 100,000 students with the support staff of less than 20 people. All of these efforts were exciting and successful. This was because I had the good fortune of working with creative and hard-working people. The success of all my professional life work is largely due to my working colleagues. I truly appreciate their dedication and hard work.

Lastly and most important, I owe a great debt of gratitude to my wife Janet, my ex-wife Erlinda, and my two daughters Michelle and Christine, for tolerating the many days I was away from home. I was not always there for special events and not being present for their daily lives, I did miss that a lot during my working days.

As I mentioned before no one is a" self-made man"! I'm certainly not one. My success was facilitated by my parents, my family , my teachers and the people that have worked with me, and the numerous individuals that influenced my life at various stages. I am grateful to all with whom I have been associated with doing my work life as well as my and social life.

Today, my wife Janet and I are enjoying our retirement in Huntington Beach, California and spending time in New Mexico vacation home. I treasure the time I spend with my daughter Christine and my daughter Michelle and her family and my three grand children Matthew and my twins Julia and Evan. All have made life's journey, most rewarding, exciting and most fulfilling!

Evan and Julia Cummings in New Mexico, Brazos Cliffs and News Mexico Clouds

SOURCES USED

2004-2014 NEW MEXICO STATE RECORD OF CENTER AND ARCHIVES

Robert Torrez: *The Tierra Amarilla Land Grant*

NASA Jet Propulsion Laboratory

National Aeronautics and Space Administration

Guillermo Lux, *Politics and Education in Hispanic New Mexico*

Sigfredo Maestas, *Children of the Normal School 60 Years in El Rito 1909-1969*

Ben Casados, Cecilia De Tucker Gonzales, Eileen Trujillo:

The Normal at El Rito An Enduring Spirit

Ross Casados

ABOUT THE AUTHOR

Benito Casados, was born in a small village of Park View, in the mountains of Northern New Mexico. He attended the local schools and graduated from Tierra Amarilla High School. He obtained his Bachelor of Science from New Mexico State University and his Master of Science from Michigan State University at Lansing, Michigan.

His career started by teaching science at Northern New Mexico College at El Rito, New Mexico. He then served as a space science specialist for eight years with NASA headquarters period for 10 years he was the director of educational services for the Jet Propulsion Laboratory in Pasadena. He was one of the founders and served as vice president for optical data Corporation the company that introduced laser disc technology into education by having the first statewide technology adoption in the state of Texas.

He served as the executive director of the Hughes electronics galaxy classroom he implemented to galaxy classroom the first nationwide interactive science and language guides television programs for elementary schools delivered nationwide by direct TV.

Ben was a founding member and board chairman of the California virtual education partners and nonprofit entity that operated five 6-12 online schools in the state of California.

Governor Deukmejian appointed Ben to the California Educational Commission in 1994. This commission created the first state wide educational technology plan for the state of California. The California Senate appointed him to the California Education Technology Council. This Council assisted school districts with their technology implementation plans. He's a member of various professional organizations.

He co-authored two books on the space shuttle with Bill Clark and authored an e-book **"A Parent Guide for Children** which includes hundreds of questions and answers commonly asked by children

And one Hispanic men's journey he describes his days going up in rule New Mexico's cents teaching career is work with NASA headquarters Jet Propulsion Laboratory and looking at him and his work as an entrepreneur

While working with NASA, he presented lectures to audiences throughout the United States being fluent in Spanish he conducted lecturing tours throughout Mexico, Central and South America and Puerto Rico. He was an adjunct professor at Oklahoma State University He wrote a syndicated column ask Andy that later evolved into his popular www.youaskandy.com a multidiscipline website that contains over 20,000 questions and answers asked by young students and encourages students to do Internet research.

Benito lives in Huntington Beach CA and spends time in their vacation home at his birthplace in Park View, now called Los Ojos, New Mexico

www.ingramcontent.com/pod-product-compliance
Lightning Source LLC
Chambersburg PA
CBHW050749100426

42744CB00012BA/1942